How To Promote YOU
With A WordPress Blog!

David Pankhurst

http://www.UtopiaMechanicus.com

To Gwen

Contents

Introduction

WordPress is a great tool for publishing your thoughts, but not everyone knows it is extremely flexible. It needn't stay an online journal. And a site built with WordPress can become just about any kind of website you need (or want). In fact, with just a little tweaking, a WordPress blog could get fantastic search engine attention for practically any business – and most especially, the business of promoting YOU!

But, WordPress needs a little extra help to put its best digital 'foot' forward to the search engines. So this book explains how to optimize your WordPress blog, how to set it up for maximum benefits for search engines (and humans), and how to use it to promote you and your business ideas. Organized around key points for online business success, I hope you'll find it a valuable reference for your online business goals!

Understand WordPress & Why It's An Incredible Tool For Online Success

One of the very first things you'll need to know about is WordPress itself – why exactly it's the best thing you've ever used for websites, and why it's a vital key to your online success!

So What Exactly Is A Blog?

Blog originally stood for "web log", and they were much like online diaries of personal events, or commentary. In them, someone might talk about their day, what happened to them, interesting thoughts (at least to them), and so forth. A blog would become a listing of these entries, organized by time, with the most recent at the top of the list, and oldest at the bottom.

Of course, after a while, and more than a few entries, it was obvious there needed to be some more order. So blogs were arranged into a listing page, with the latest articles, or blog posts, placed in reverse chronological order. And older entries would extend onto other web pages, as many as needed for the posts. Finally, posts were organized into categories, so visitors could quickly find all the blogger's musings about cats, as opposed to dogs and fishies.

That's the start: But over time, people realized the programs that managed these website web logs (by now shortened just to blogs) were useful for other things.

After all, they asked, why do the articles have to be personal? Couldn't they be anything? And why do the articles have to be in chronological order? In fact, if you lost the date and time display for each article post (called the time stamp), then you just had a regular website, with one main page showing the most recent information, and other pages scattered around the website, where the other articles lay.

In fact in 2005, when I wrote the first edition of this book, I realized you could use a blog for just about any type of site. With only a few adjustments, the way a blog managed daily musings was almost exactly the way regular websites managed their pages of information.

Not only that, but the programs that managed these blogs were growing in power month by month. In fact, by 2005/2006, tools like WordPress had made it easier to manage a regular site with a blog program, than by running it with most any other tool!

For example, when I first started online in 1996, I had to create every web page by hand by writing HTML, the actual code that describes the layout and design of the page.

Besides being error–prone, changes were painful. If I wanted to add a new page of text, I would have to check over all other pages on the site, and then add links for them to the new page. Plus, adding a search box to my site (now a common feature) required complicated software I could never get to work right – so I didn't add it.

The result was very slow changes, and on the Internet, change is one of the absolutely best ways to get attention and visitors (stale sites are like stale bread – you can recycle them into another meal, but they are uninteresting as they are!)

Now, fast–forward to today, and look at a tool like WordPress, that popular free program for managing a blog on your site:

• I log into my website, and type out a page of text just like using a word processor, where I can write anything I want. But most importantly, I just write the text; I don't put in the web page code, because that's separate. And so I don't have to worry about my website design, and programming it, when I write any more. In fact, with WordPress, I can change my website's design with a single button press, and experiment with the 'look' to my heart's content!

• When I'm done writing, I simply press the Publish button, and a new page appears on my site, all perfectly formatted and laid out.

• It even takes care of all the linking. Old blog pages have a link automatically to my new page, and my new page links to all of them. That means that visitors (and search engines) everywhere on my site see that new link to that new page, and can visit it – without me worrying.

• And at last I have my search engine! Instead of a complicated program I always had to fiddle with to get working (poorly), WordPress has one built in, so visitors can look up specific words on my site, and find articles easily – even my newest one – again, automatically!

The fact of the matter is this: Blog programs like WordPress are designed to make it easy to let the world know about pages of writing. And that's exactly what you want from a regular website as well!

A Side Benefit: RSS Feeds

If a program like WordPress only took care of your website, it would be a useful tool. But it does so much more. And one of those things is creating RSS feeds, another powerful traffic tool.

A feed is (technically) an XML document of the text content of a website. It is possible to include images and other things, like video and music, or even more advanced formats, such as for streaming video, or podcasting. However, these are exceptions: The majority of sites use text–only RSS feeds.

To understand how useful RSS feeds are, imagine if you wanted to explain your site to someone. You might discuss the layout, the color, the types of buttons you used – but more than likely, it's the text of each article that would describe the meat of the site best.

That's an RSS Feed: A listing that grabs the article text and makes it available in a format that's minus the lovely design, great color scheme, and cool buttons. And whereas this doesn't seem worthwhile (and a trifle rude, since people are missing your site's eye–catching layout), there are some very good reasons for it:

• An RSS feed is easily readable by computers, which helps make it popular (and popular can equal traffic and visitors to your site). For example, some sites grab other site's feeds and repackage them for display on their site. If they then include the article links back to your site (which they legally should do), this may help build search engine rankings.

• An RSS Feed saves a tremendous amount for space. On the Internet, a picture isn't worth 1,000 words, it's more often 25,000 – and leaving all the graphics out of a website and putting just the text in an RSS feed means those visitors are not grabbing huge chunks of your site's bandwidth unnecessarily. It's also faster, and faster means viewers are less likely to get bored and give up reading.

• This streamlined viewing is also a benefit for potential markets. If you've ever heard of a Feed Reader, it's a program or service that gathers multiple feeds from sites, and groups them together for you to read easily. So rather than individually visiting each site and checking for new posts, a feed reader can automatically check dozens (or hundreds) of sites, and give you the latest information. Most importantly for you, the RSS feed you create automatically via WordPress is the perfect 'bait' if you're trying to attract these RSS feed reader type folks.

In fact, some may argue that it was RSS feeds that made blogs as popular as they are today. At one point, people were certain that feeds were going to replace email. It didn't happen, but a great many people still rely on that RSS text for their "daily fix" of blog information.

One final point about feeds: Since they can become the 'meat' of your website, it's possible that people need never visit your site after that first time to initialize (activate) the feed in their feed reader program. So, you may wish to limit what they can grab remotely. We'll look into the pros and cons of limiting your feed (and how to manage it) in a later section, but for now, understand that a feed is a 'lite' version of your website text – and a powerful promotional tool.

But while feeds can be a mixed blessing for traffic, there's another blog–related item that is all golden – and it even pings like gold...

Ping, Ping, Ping – I'm Home!

The blog ping gets its name from the old submarine 'ping', a sonar tone which was made to hear if something was out there. Later on, a web programmer created a tool that 'pinged' sites, a very fast and efficient Internet message to check if a site existed – if they heard back, the site was available.

WordPress and other blog tools took the concept of pinging and reversed it: Instead of a ping to see if anyone was out there, they used it to announce to the world THEY existed! To understand this way of using it, just think of those submarine movies, where a sonar ping accidentally gives away the position of the good guy's sub to the bad guys.

For example, when I write a new post on my blog and publish it (make it visible to the world on my website), the WordPress program will 'ping' a list of sites to let them know the article now exists. These notification sites track what blogs are publishing; more importantly, search engines pay special attention to these sites, and so pinging is a quick way to get noticed by them. The result is that the article announcement you made "out there" gets you attention. In fact, perhaps they would have been better calling it 'crowing' instead of pinging, since it's more like announcing you've done something wonderful, and then hoping people come by to see what you've done and pat you on the back!

Not every site can understand a ping, and not every site does something useful when they get a ping, so to make it easier, people created something called a "ping list", which is a list of site URLs that do accept pings, and understand the ping message. WordPress can use any list you wish to give it, and pings the URLs when a new post is published; however, it comes with a built–in ping list, so you don't have to add to it.

Now from a blog's point of view, that ping announces a new post. So it didn't take long for search engines to take notice of these ping sites and give them extra attention, since it made their work of discovering new web pages easier. Which of course made pinging these sites a great way to get noticed by the search engines. Soon, not only were legitimate blogs sending out the "here am I with fresh writing" ping signal, but other programs and sites were too – and not always for fresh content. Many people found that if they 'pinged' often, they'd get noticed by the search engines – and possibly improve their search engine rankings, and get more traffic for their sites.

You can guess the next step: Search engines caught on they were being fooled, and took steps to catch the worst offenders, penalizing them severely (in some cases, dropping search engine listings for their sites).

Since then many have backed off from too–frequent pinging. "Blog and ping" products are less common than once upon a time. Of course, pinging is still extremely valuable, but sites are becoming more careful as to their pinging, doing it when posting new content instead of more frequently. As with many things, pinging is beneficial in moderation, but don't abuse it. Fortunately, your blog will take care of that automatically once you have it set up.

But for a typical blog (and blogs set up for business), if you ping from time to time when you have something new, you can expect search engines to hear about you – and in a way that a normal site can't match, because regular HTML sites don't 'ping'!

The Human Element: Comments

If you've ever visited a blog, you've likely read the comments there. With few exceptions, for every post there is an opportunity for anyone to add their opinion or view. And that is a huge traffic boon, for the simplest of reasons: Humans like attention.

For example, I recently had someone call me up for a telephone survey. Now I hate giving out personal details, and so do many other people, because identify theft is a very real danger nowadays. Yet these companies keep calling people, and thrive in this day and age – all because many people still do want to give out their personal views (and details). And blogs are an ideal way to do so online.

If your blog includes the ability to comment on posts (and not all should – yet another feature we'll delve into later), then you can see how this would build traffic and success:

• You increase traffic. People not only post their comments, they revisit to see how others have responded. Notice on many blogs how the same people will comment back and forth on a topic – and each of these is a return visit to the site. Not only that, but many, many, other people are lurking around and reading it all without commenting, accounting for further traffic (think of each commenter as the tip of the iceberg, traffic–wise).

• As people comment on your posts repeatedly, you build a community. That community can be valuable as support, and income.

• Comments form extra content on your website, and search engines love content like this. After all, how often have you searched Google and been sent to a specific comment on a web page, instead of the main article itself? So as you build up more comments for your articles, you build up more search engine 'reach'.

Of course, comments have a dark (spammy) side, and we'll touch on that later. But if you decide to go this route, you can see some great results from accepting comments on your site.

However, not all the benefits of WordPress are traffic related. There is a feature of WordPress that is a boon to busy webmasters everywhere – dynamic pages.

Phantom Web Pages And Dynamic Sites

As I mentioned already, an old-style website often contained dozens of web pages, sometimes thousands, all of which needed to be maintained. These sites were called static, since the information stayed unchanging on them until you made physical adjustments to the files.

For a site like that, maintenance was excruciating: Imagine a 5,000 page static website, like a store, and the changes you'd go through to add a new product!

However, people eventually caught on to dynamic web pages (and websites). That is, rather than a physical web page existing somewhere on the website service (called a webhost), somewhat like a file on your hard drive, you could create a single page with a little bit of programming. In turn, that program could be 'run' each time someone visited your site, serving up a web page right there and then. From the visitor's point of view, they see a regular web page. From the website's point of view, however, that page is brand new, cobbled together like a short–order cook's meal from scratch, and served piping hot.

WordPress is one of those programs. There are of course many others, proof of just how popular this "dynamic page" system is. And it should be – there's big benefits in creating your web pages exactly when you need them, and not before:

• The 'look' of the website can be streamlined to a single file or group of files. For example, WordPress groups the design of a website into a small collection of files, called a theme. Switch the theme with a button press from within WordPress, and your site magically (and instantly) changes its look – everywhere on the site, for every web page – instantly.

• New and changing content is easily handled. WordPress manages how the pages appear from start to finish. And it can add new links, changes in text, and everything else that makes up a normal web page without extra effort, since it's creating these pages right when they are needed.

• Likewise, last minute editorial changes can be snuck in. Static versus dynamic web pages are like the newspaper versus television: Trying to put "breaking news" into a newspaper meant waiting until the next press run, whereas TV news can interrupt anything, anytime.

• And while a program like WordPress puts together the basic web page as it's needed, it can do much more. In fact, there is a whole industry of mini–programs that attach themselves to WordPress (called plugins and widgets) that add extra features. Like those gadgets and trimmings for your car, these can be for show, or for real benefits. And you can quickly add or remove them, knowing WordPress will display them along with any web page, and without any fuss, the benefit of dynamic web pages.

So dynamic pages are the best thing ever, right? Almost. They do come at a price, since the website has to run the WordPress program to create the web page each and every time someone visits. Like a waiter in a quiet restaurant, you can get that extra service now, but if things get busy, something will suffer. On very popular websites, the extra effort of creating these pages can cripple a site, unless you take steps to avoid it (and of course, there's a trick to preventing that which we'll cover later on!)

So What Exactly Is WordPress?

As you can see, WordPress is a very handy tool for a variety of things – so what is this tool really, and why is it so popular?

Firstly, WordPress is a program that runs on your website, serving up dynamic web pages when people request them. But in fact it's a bit more technical than that.

On the Internet, web page viewing is done by HTML 'requests', where your Internet browser sends a message asking for specific content, like web pages (it can also ask for images, or a whole slew of other Internet content, but we'll stick with web pages in this example). These Internet connections from your browser program talk to the website, which in reality are also programs, called servers, running on remote computers (naturally, since they "serve up" things on the Internet).

For many computers out there, that server program is called Apache, and the computer it is part of runs a variation of Linux (or sometimes BSD or Solaris, all based on the Granddaddy operating system Unix developed around 1970).

That server takes an Internet request and processes it. How it does that exactly depends on the way the server is set up. For example, when using WordPress on the server, the request for a web page is transferred to WordPress. However, WordPress is written in PHP (a programming language), so first PHP has to be activated, then WordPress has to be activated, then the web page's request can be processed. That resulting dynamic web page is then passed to the server, which passes it to the

---

browser that requested it, thus giving the visitor the warm feeling of having visited a site (even if the site is really created by a computer program or two).

There's even another layer stuck in there: Apache doesn't just automatically call WordPress (it doesn't even understand what a 'WordPress' is!) Instead, it's designed to look at a specific file on a specific part of its hard drive. WordPress sets up that special file (called .htaccess) with information to pull a slight–of–hand, so all real requests for web pages (files) are turned into fake requests, directed to WordPress. Apache thinks it's looking for a single file, and gets a whole program!

So WordPress handles the fake–out with Apache (or other servers, such as with Windows). It also manages all your blog pages, blog design, and interconnections. It gives you pings, XML feeds, and makes it easy to add content to your site. Plus, it's a PHP program. Anything else?

Yes – it's Open Source. If you've never heard of Open Source, it's a movement to create software that can be looked into by anyone, much like reading a book (a very, very, dry book, that is). Unlike many software programs, where you can't look at the actual product internals (called source code) unless you're a programmer for the company that makes it, Open Source prides itself on visibility. The benefits are that program problems (nicknamed bugs) are often caught and fixed rapidly, since popular programs get popular, even worldwide, attention.

And with WordPress, Open Source also means Free – so you get the tremendous power of this product at a price that makes it very simple to use (and reuse, since you pay nothing for as many sites as you put WordPress on).

Popularity brings another side benefit with it – help. While not every Open Source project gets hundreds of thousands of users, when it does, you get a lot of ready support, and plenty of information on using it (just do an Internet search on 'WordPress' and see what comes up).

So this means you aren't left high and dry if there's a problem. In fact, you can't throw a rock without hitting a WordPress 'expert' these days! And while you may have to be careful whom you work with, there's certainly no lack of people willing to help you get the most out of your future WordPress website.

As you can see, WordPress provides some pretty strong positives, so much so that it's just about cleared the playing field of other competitors. However, one other still remains, and it's a biggy: Blogger.com, owned by Google.

Blogger Vs WordPress: Who Wins?

In this corner, a huge behemoth managed by one of the largest tech companies in the world. In the other corner, a small group of people tinkering with an Open Source program. Who wins?

In a nutshell: WordPress.

While I find Blogger.com has some benefits, there's very real reasons to avoid it for your website:

• Google owns, and controls, Blogger. There are reports of people losing their sites overnight because of problems (in all fairness, these are because of violations of Google's Terms of Service, and well within their right). However, it means that whatever you write on Blogger has the potential to be removed without warning, so I strongly recommend keeping a backup copy of everything. At the very least, everything you write should be on your home computer, and then from there copied to your Blogger blog.

• Although Blogger is flexible, you can't go under the hood and tinker. In contrast, WordPress code is on your own site, and is yours to tinker with to your heart's content. While many won't dig into PHP and the programming code at the core of WordPress, you can get add–ons that give more flexibility to the blog (called widgets and plugins), and that require no programming knowledge to run.

Not all is black however: Blogger has its own advantages, and I do recommend a Blogger.com blog for some people. The main reason is that it's an easy beginning. Unlike WordPress, which requires you have a site to set it up on, Blogger is run (hosted) on Google's servers – so you could have a blog up and running in a few minutes.

However, as you learn blogs and blogging, you will want to move to WordPress because of the greater control it gives you.

You might wonder: Does a blog on Blogger.com benefit from Google ownership, as far as search engine listings go? It might seem smart to have a Blogger.com blog for search engine visibility, since Google owns the site. However, the fact of the matter is that Google is in the business of quality search results. So if Blogger.com blogs gave people an unfair advantage, they'd be giving up a long term goal (Masters of Search) for a short term one (popularize Blogger.com). I think they are smart enough to realize how quickly people would turn on them if they showed a bias like that. In fact, a quick check of Google's search engine results shows Blogger.com blogs are just that: As good and as bad as any other website. It's what you put on it that counts.

The "Other Brother" – WordPress.com

When I mentioned WordPress had only one real competitor, I was talking about other companies. In fact, WordPress does have some more competition besides Blogger.com – itself.

When you are first introduced to WordPress, it can be confusing. That's because there are two distinct flavors of WordPress that people commonly use, based on how they work:

• A hosted version, found at WordPress.com, where every– and any– body can set up a blog free of charge.

• A self hosted version, which you put on your own website. This one consists of a group of files you download from WordPress.org

To avoid confusion, here's how to tell WordPress.com and WordPress.org apart. WordPress.com is just like Blogger.com – you pick a name, get a blog, and start writing. WordPress.org is where you get the tools to put WordPress on your own site. It's like building a computer from parts, or buying a ready made one from Walmart. So why use one over the other?

• In a word, control. WordPress.com, like Blogger.com, has strict rules on how your blog can be used and maintained. For example, any advertising is frowned on, and even AdSense (a common form of monetizing your site) is prohibited on most blogs (this is in contrast with Blogger.com, where some advertising is allowed, in particular

Google's own AdSense).

• Like Blogger.com, you are at the mercy of another site. It is possible to have your site deleted, leaving you with nothing. All the effort and care spent developing a website can be gone overnight if you break their rules.

• WordPress.org on the other hand provides a product you place on your site, and that you control. And with that control you also have the opportunity to make money – big money – something that would close your site in a hurry on WordPress.com

• Of course, with power comes complexity: Hosting your own blog is easy, but not nearly as easy as letting someone else do it for you! So some have decided to go the WordPress.com route.

• Additionally, for beginners unused to WordPress, getting a blog on WordPress.com is an easy way to take the program out for a spin without investing in a whole website setup. You don't have to do anything useful with it even – just sign up and play around.

I like WordPress.com, but I can't recommend you grab a blog there, aside from playing with it. The fact is, WordPress is free software that lets you do things "your way". What better way to maximize it than by putting it on your own site, and managing it from there, where the sky is (practically) the limit?

And in fact, one big benefit of hosting your own blog (as maintaining it on your own website is called) is the power to make it decidedly UN–bloglike if you want...

To Be, Or Not To Be, A Blog

As I mentioned earlier, not all blog features suit a regular site. For example, I don't always want people to know the date and time of a post, and I don't always want comments. As well, many themes include a header I find annoying (too much space wasted at the top, too big a blog title, poor graphic choice, etc.)

For a regular website, any customizing is a pain, since changes have to repeated on dozens or even hundreds of static web pages. But for a WordPress site, small changes can alter the whole site's look completely, making the blog look more like a 'regular' website.

For example, at one time WordPress only had the main page that was the blog list, a listing of all the most recent posts, sometimes in a summarized (excerpted) form.

Now, WordPress allows you to move that to another section of your blog, and make the main page a fixed post (or page, which is what WordPress calls these types of web pages). This means your main page where the blog rests can look more like a regular website, perhaps with a welcoming message, or sales text.

Throughout this guide, you'll hear a number of similar blog terms that mean quite different things. Here's the minimum you need to know:

Posts are those articles that appear chronologically, with a date stamp (usually), and on a normal WordPress blog appear on the front page (called the Home or the Home Page) in a list.

Pages, in contrast, have no date, and are used for fixed content, like an About page, or a Contact page.

There's other differences between Posts and Pages: Posts send out a ping when published, while Pages do not. As well, you can organize posts on your blog according to categories, whereas the Posts are not organized that way (but can be used for the WordPress Menu system listings, for example).

And to further muddle things up, you'll also hear about web pages, a generic term for ANY item on a blog website, including (but not limited to) posts OR pages. And website? It actually can refer to anything on your web server, not just a WordPress blog (and obviously, a web page isn't limited to a blog, either); however, in this guide you can assume we mean a blog web page and a blog website whenever they are mentioned, unless otherwise explained. Keep these terms in mind as you dive into the terminology of WordPress, and you'll have no problems.

Categories allow another kind of flexibility. For example, you could use different categories to group posts regarding different products. The result would be an easy to maintain FAQ (Frequently Asked Questions) on your product line, instead of the "here's what I did today" style posts of the usual blog.

Important also to making a blog look different is using those powerful add–ons to WordPress: Themes, plugins and widgets. Themes can radically change the look of your blog, and even how parts are displayed (you'd work with the theme if you wished to remove the time stamp for each post, for instance). As well, a theme manages how sections of the blog look, so you could have different styles for different parts of the site; even wide differences, like a vibrant page for one category, and a subdued one for another.

Plugins and widgets add to that flexibility. Plugins add power behind the scenes for the most part, whereas widgets are more visual items, and appear on the sidebar of the blog web page (usually).

Between themes, plugins, and widgets, there is a tremendous amount of range available for your blog. And the good news is that if there's a real need for something, the WordPress community is so vast that someone quite likely has already thought of it and written it out there – yet another benefit of a huge pool of fans.

But there's one last benefit of WordPress, a biggy – and the main reason you're holding this book in your hands now...

Hi Ho, It's Off To SEO We Go

Search engines like those of Google, Microsoft and Yahoo are fickle beasties. They will grab anything and everything on the web that they can; yet sometimes they seem to just nibble a bit here and there, and other times they gobble a website down whole.

There is a large industry trying to read the mind of the big search engines, and for good reason: The company that can promise (and really deliver) top search listings would be incredibly rich.

But as much as companies want to understand the mind of Google (and Yahoo and Bing), the search engines are trying at least as hard to muddy the waters, to make sure that everyone can benefit with good, solid content, and that no one can 'game' the system to get preferred treatment; that is, top listings with anything but top content.

That's the bad news. The good news is that while the search engines work hard to keep the playing field level, people like you and me can still get noticed. But it's not a slam dunk. It takes a knowledge of SEO.

SEO is an acronym for Search Engine Optimization (or Optimized). It refers to making a website or web page as accessible as possible to search engines, with the goal of ranking higher in the listings for certain phrases. Simply put, if your site uses the same words that potential customer type in when searching, the search engines just might help you out by showing them your site.

When I first started working with WordPress, I was struck by how "un–SEO" the design was. For example, the HTML in the basic theme was only somewhat helpful for search engines, but other SEO features were missing completely (more on these in later chapters). The result was that a few 'tricks' were needed to maximize the WordPress blog for search engine success – and the first edition of this guide was born in 2005.

SEO is not a trivial topic. Simply put, good SEO equals Success. Here's why:

• The higher you rank in the search engines, the more likely searchers will find you. And if you don't think high page rankings matter that much, ask yourself: How often do you go to page 50 (or even 5, or 2) in Google when searching for something?

• SEO is not just optimizing, but useful optimizing. Anyone can 'promise' you high rankings for useless terms and phrases. But if no one looks for those phrases, the rankings are useless as well. So SEO must focus on practical items, keywords that matter to your target market.

• Search engines open the door to you as you improve your focus. Once a search engine can pigeonhole you and your site, then it knows where to place you for maximum benefit (for itself of course – after all, Google's goal is to be a better Google, with better search results, not help you out!) With this focus, the search engines can rate you more effectively. For example, Google has what it calls PageRank, a rating of how 'good' your site is. If they score you high, they will visit more often, pay more attention to what you have to say, and bump up your rankings in the search engines. So as you strive to get better, they reward you by helping you out.

To put it in a nutshell, a basic WordPress blog still needs work to maximize its search engine optimization, and this book gives you the details on how to do just that for your site. Once you've read and applied them, you'll find that your site is far more 'digestible' by the search engines. And by making their job easier, they're apt to return the favor, and help you gain those all–important search engine rankings.

I expect you can understand now why I really like WordPress, and why it's the perfect tool for many sites. I hope you agree, because with this powerful tool, you too can build a powerful website.

But before we go and build that blog, it's time to analyze – what exactly do YOU want to do with it?

Focus Single–Minded On Your Goal – Why You NEED A Website

Today, you can't NOT have a website.

Why?

Think of a website as a business card – and then think bigger:

• Can a business card provide 24/7 information and support?

• What about preselling clients without those long sales calls?

• Can you build a relationship with people over time using just a business card?

All these are possible with a website – and much easier than with a 3x5 business card!

The reason is that every article you put online – every sentence – every word – gets indexed into the search engines (especially when, as we've seen, you use a WordPress blog). And these words can involve your company, your product, or any information you consider vital.

From there, potential clients ask the search engine questions, and if these questions are relevant to your site, the search engines list you as a likely source. They click on a link, go to your site, and you now have a great chance to convert that potential client into an actual client.

Make no mistake: Search engine traffic is incredibly cheap traffic (among the cheapest) and you can get it from just opening up a blog. And all that traffic can bring you clients and sales, a great result from converting visitors into profitable traffic.

As a promotional tool extraordinaire, a website/blog packs a powerful punch. And how you style that site for maximum impact, and what you put on it, is the topic of this trick.

Go Digital!

It sounds grand – open up a website, and make endless riches selling something that costs nothing to make, forever and ever. In fact, some people have made very, very, good money selling 'bits', digital information that costs little or nothing to make and distribute.

For instance, when I wrote the first edition of this book, it was a short guide that I published online using a format called Acrobat PDF (a very portable digital format, readable on many types of computers). With just a bit of free promotion, the first month alone was upwards of $10,000 in sales – yet there were no costs at all per copy, since the digital information was virtually free to reproduce and deliver.

However, despite a success like that, reality is a little different for most, and it pays to think things through with a new idea:

• Just because ONE item can succeed doesn't mean EVERY item will. Talk to any online developer, and you'll likely hear more tales of the product or service that didn't make it than the ones that did.

• Nothing is truly free, although the cost can be vanishingly small. For example, Payment processors (like PayPal) take their percentage, as do distributors like eBay. Also, you use up bandwidth delivering a product (this refers to the transmission rate and capacity of the Internet connection, which can be large, but does cost). Plus, there are development costs, since few things today are developed for free. Of course, when a product sells at a high enough price, and in large enough quantities, these other costs grow less and less important.

• Low cost equals easy imitations. A problem on the Internet is that once someone has a new idea, it's very easy for others to duplicate it, and often cheaper (since research and development has already been done). Within that first year or so, I saw brand new 'experts' explain how to optimize WordPress, many referring to techniques I originally discussed.

• As well, since there are countries out there where the cost of living is much lower than North America, competition on the Internet is a very real thing, especially for digital items. It would be almost impossible to print and sell books for the average person in Uganda for example, but with access to a computer, they could easily publish the same information online at little or no cost, and make money.

Now this isn't meant to scare you. It's simply to point out that many people have a rosy picture of the Internet, and aren't aware of all sides. Yes, you can make a huge amount of money with little more than an idea. But it's not always straightforward, so it pays to spend some time to really analyze what you want to put out on the Internet.

Yes, WordPress CAN Do That

WordPress is the key to getting online. A website is within your grasp. So now the question is – what will you DO with it? With the whole wide world of online activity out there, where best to head off to find fame and fortune online?

The fact is, you do need a reason to go online. It's tempting to start something "just to do it", but it's expensive to try project after project without results. Granted, the Internet makes it very inexpensive to try (and you do learn things as you try, even if you fail), but you save time and effort by focusing on the target, and hitting the bulls–eye first time out.

This is important to deal with because, as bullish as I am about WordPress, it is just a tool, a way to manage your website. It won't come up with the product, or style the site to suit – you'll have to do that. The first step is determining what you want a site to do for you, so let's take a look at what a blog will need for any site.

What's A Blog Made Of, Anyway?

If you looked at a typical blog, you might not at first recognize it as a different type of site at all.

However, looks can be deceiving. In fact, a lot goes on behind the scenes:

• First you have WordPress, the program which 'runs' your website as a blog. We've already seen how much it does for your site.

• Then, you have the actual appearance of the blog, which is determined by a theme, that special design code to make the generic WordPress display mold into any style you want. It's this theme that makes a WordPress blog so versatile as a website.

• But even before you set up on your website, you need to stake a claim on the Internet. For example, your blog will not go just anywhere: It will need a domain name, and you'll need a physical place to 'rest' your site, called web hosting.

• And there's more: The blog can be filled with anything, but of course you're better off putting vital information there (at least, vital to your success). That information is usually grouped under the generic term 'content', and can vary from informational articles to personal blog posts to anything else you may feel like writing about.

• And last but not least, there is maintenance. Every website needs a little TLC now and then. You may need to deal with email. A server upgrade may mean taking a look at your site to make sure everything still works. Even WordPress needs upgrading from time to time. And no matter how nice your theme is, there will come a time you'll probably want a new design.

As you can see, a blog requires managing a fair amount of details, and careful planning like any website. For that reason, it's important to have a good idea what your site will do, and what you expect of it, right from the start. Like building a house, the foundation will determine a great deal of how the house will look, so you do well to look at the foundation of your website and goals before you start designing your online 'home'.

Over the years when I've explained the reasons for a website, I've grouped them into several main categories. Most sites fall into one of the first three; quite likely, they'll cover what you want to do online as well.

Reason #1 – A Website to Promote Your Business, Service, Or Product

This is the most common reason for a website or blog – to promote your company and what you have to offer. And in this WordPress excels.

For example, you can set up a theme design that looks much like other business sites. Instead of dated blog posts, you can leave off the dates, then write articles and scatter them throughout the site as content. Directed content on a business topic is something search engines love to index, helping attract people interested in your product and service.

For instance, if you sell vacuum cleaners, articles on maintenance, trading in, how they work, pollution, ratings, and more are all things people are interested in. And that content can draw people to your site, and help establish you as THE company to deal with for vacuums.

In creating the design of the site, you'll want to keep money–making in the forefront. While some big sites can just be "out there" and expect that to be enough promotion for them, you should plan to try to make money off of every visitor (called monetizing). For that reason, your site likely will have:

• A contact form, where people can reach your service team or sales staff with questions, whether by email, postal mail (nicknamed "snail mail" online), or phone/fax.

• A newsletter or email list signup form, since email lists of potential clients can be very profitable.

• A FAQ (Frequently Asked Questions) section, where you can offload some (or all) of your technical support by showing answers online, and letting visitors browse and solve common problems on their own.

• A sales section, where you actually can take orders for your product(s).

• Time–relevant sections, such as banners or notices of limited–time sales or offers.

The good news is this is all very simple with WordPress, using free products (plugins) and a bit of programming.

As an example, at one time long ago I offered this book as a downloadable report, along with others on technical subjects, via a customized WordPress blog. From that site, visitors could look at each product's sales page, then scroll to the bottom and order. Because the product was digital (that Adobe Acrobat PDF format I mentioned earlier), I could offer it to buyers right after purchase for download. Of course, if your site offers a tangible (non–digital) item, then you may need different methods to sell and deliver, such as a credit card order form, or a telephone number for phone orders.

The benefits of a site like this is you can get online quickly and take orders (and make money) immediately – all with an approachable and relevant company site. For many companies, a business sales site is quite straightforward with WordPress; and as a bonus, once set up, it's easy to manage.

That's one main reason for a site, but here's another...

Reason #2 – A Website To Promote Yourself

Try this: Go to Google, and type in any famous person you can think of. I'll bet they have a blog. Perhaps it's rarely updated, and maybe not even written by themselves, but they'll have one (plus dozens of other blogs put up there by fans).

Why? Because a blog gives search engines a place to go for relevant content – in this case, relevant about them! And that search engine attention can work for you too when you're just starting out.

Imagine you plan to be the next Tony Robbins. You can give lots of inspirational seminars locally, but millions and billions of people will not know of you outside your home city.

Yet with a blog, once searchers have a name, they have a website. And you decide what they read, and what the focus is. For example, if you have your own "success system" to go with that Tony Robbins dream, then you can document it there, give examples of how it works, and encourage people to apply it in their lives.

Using a site like that, people read what you have to say, and thereby get to know you. And despite never having met you, they can form a relationship from a distance (something TV and film stars have counted on for decades), and that relationship can motivate them to act – buy your tapes and books, invite you to come speak, whatever you wish.

Now in this example we're talking about becoming a self–help guru. What if instead you wished to promote yourself as an author? Even easier, since the writings on your blog are the writings you want to promote. One of the biggest problems with succeeding as an author is getting enough people to want to buy your published book. With a blog, you get attention for free while you write, building up interest and readers. Then you can go to a publisher with a ready–made pool of potential buyers – a huge plus in getting a book deal! There are many examples of bloggers turned published writers – just search on "blogger turned author" for sites and examples.

So whether you're promoting yourself for a book, for a motivational job, or for just about anything, a personalized (and personal) blog gives you a way to reach people – and build up an audience. In turn, these visitors can become your future customers.

No business? Not interested (or too shy) to promote yourself? There's still a third common way people use blogs to get ahead.

Reason #3 – A Website To Promote Someone (Or Something) Else

If you've been online for any amount of time, you may have heard of the term "affiliate marketing". With a website like this, you first get traffic in using a variety of techniques, such as advertising or writing. Then, this flow of visitors is pitched a product (or products) on your site, and go elsewhere to buy it. The money is made from your commission for the sale, as an affiliate of that product. In effect, your website has become a commission–only salesman.

At first glance, it might not seem too valuable to sell someone else's products instead of something you own yourself. However, there are pros and cons with this system:

• If you have no product of your own, but visitors to your site, offering other people's products can make use of this traffic for immediate cash.

• It's not always "all or nothing" with commissions: While some offer money only when there is a purchase, others pay just to send traffic to them. One of the biggest, Google AdSense, places ads on your site, and then pays you if anyone clicks to visit the client's page.

• Becoming a commissioned middleman means you don't need to develop, test, maintain, build, troubleshoot, or update a product of your own; so it can be very stress free compared to other kinds of websites.

• However, being a middleman means you compete with other salesman, each of which could potentially take the lead (and the bulk of sales) away from you.

• Of course, since you're not tied down to your own product, you're free to change products, or even offer multiple ones. This could lead to making even more money with little extra effort.

This last point is the key to the popularity of affiliate sites: You're not limited to setting up one site. In fact, there are untold numbers of products out there, and many people make a business of setting up dozens (or hundreds) of blogs on specific topics, and then promoting tied–in products on those sites. For instance, a site may provide hair care tips, and then offer links for hair care products. If each site makes even a few dollars a day in commissions, dozens of sites can quickly add up. And with companies like eBay and Google eager to pay you to send traffic (and buyers) to them, there are a lot of topics you can create affiliate websites on!

Others Reasons For Websites

As I said, these three are the top reasons I recommend a website: Promoting your business or service, promoting you, and promoting others via affiliate commissions.

Is that all? No; for example, you could simply place a one page website online as a business card, just to let the world know you exist (some companies actually do little more than this). But the problem with that is there's no goal, no purpose to it, so you're wasting valuable Internet real estate without a clear benefit. In the end, you're better off using it to promote your company or yourself actively, and getting some advantage from the search engines coming by for a visit. For that reason, I recommend every site you build tries to promote something: You, your product/business, or someone else's products.

Not convinced? Perhaps you plan to actually work with WordPress as a designer, programmer, installer, etc. Of course, in that case your blog is a "calling card" for your abilities. But the fact of the matter is, you are doing the same thing as already mentioned: Either promoting yourself (designer, installer, etc.) or promoting your business (working with WordPress in many forms), so everything I've already said applies to you. Why not then focus on promotion, and make that website profitable for you?

Still, what about brand awareness? Some companies feel they only need to get their name out there. But frankly, while companies like IBM and Microsoft can spend millions on building brand awareness without asking for something in return, you can't afford to do so.

So make your website do more than be a placeholder. Think hard about what you want your website to accomplish, its purpose. And to track how well your site is doing what it should, you need specific goals.

So How Will YOU Measure Success?

In putting a website online, you're spending time and money getting your message out there. To make sure the money is well spent, you must track what it does, and its results. That means you must measure what your 'success' is, which varies for different sites.

For example, a business blog can measure its success with sales made via the website (or via phone or fax, if they are able to track which orders came from online visitors).

There, improving their website will lead to more sales, and is a very real goal for success.

Likewise, if you are making money from affiliates, a dollar value can tell you how well you're doing. Changing products you promote, adding content to your site, buying traffic through advertising, all lead to specific dollar amounts you can track.

But what about other sites, like those that promote yourself? How do you track success for them?

For sites like that, another measurement besides money is vital. For example, you may build up a list of people who want an email from you, that is, who have joined your email list. The size of that list, and how fast it is increasing, can be a great indicator of how you're doing.

Another benefit of an email list is that these people can be turned into customers at a later date; for example, when you eventually have a book. And even if you don't have a product of your own yet, you might occasionally mention other company's products, get a commission from sales, and thereby turning your self–promoting blog into an affiliate blog!

But even an email list doesn't have to be your metric to test and improve. It's also possible to track visitors alone. Perhaps you are looking to influence people via your online writing. In that case, with enough visitors, you can offer advertising and make money from your writing directly (again, affiliate sales). There, your goal for success is high amounts of traffic, and your content would be written to get the right people, and lots of them, to drop by frequently.

So no matter what site you put together, success means something to you. Spend some time figuring out what it is, and then determine to go for it. And keep at it, because there's something even more important than knowing your goals – it's STAYING with them.

> What exactly is an email list? Although we'll discuss it in more detail later on in the book, they are not unfamiliar. Likely you've joined one (or several), offering your email address to a company so they can send you news, offers, and such things. From your point of view, you get information you want; from the company's point of view, they have a

reader they can contact again and again for free, and who might eventually buy. Also, many companies email their list with relevant information frequently (such as weekly), helping to create a relationship, which in turn improves the chance of a purchase in the future. And the money involved is not trivial: Many marketers estimate a subscriber on their list as being worth ten cents to a dollar in sales per month (on average), so even a smallish list of 5,000 people can earn from $6,000 to $60,000 dollars a year for a business if cultivated properly!

A Word About Persistence

If you're just starting out with a site, that's great – the next section will cover many of the basic nuts and bolts of starting up, from figuring out a domain name, to which hosting is reputable, to actually working with WordPress.

However, one caution: It's important to estimate carefully how much work you'll need to get things done. I find that especially with newer ones and blogging, the effort and time involved in keeping it going is unexpected. It's very easy to bite off more than you can chew, and end up with a half–finished project, in this case a website without enough done on it to bring in visitors.

I'm not saying this to discourage you from setting up a website or blog. However, the Internet is littered with sites that were started and then let to lie fallow soon after. It's far better to plan to do less and end up doing more, than the reverse.

And in creating a site, one thing you'll need more than any tech help or training – persistence. A client once shared with me with these words from US president Calvin Coolidge regarding persistence:

> *"Nothing in this world can take the place of persistence. Talent will not; nothing is more common than unsuccessful people with talent. Genius will not; unrewarded genius is almost a proverb. Education will not; the world is full of educated derelicts. Persistence and determination alone are omnipotent. The slogan 'press on' has solved and always will solve the problems of the human race."*

Oddly enough, his advice on follow through is even more vital today that in his day. Why?

In the 1920s, any endeavor was a lot of work, whether it was setting up a shop, running a farm, delivering newspapers, or in fact any money–making enterprise.

Today, with tools like WordPress, it's incredibly easy to set up a business. I can go from an idea to a finished website in under a day if I wanted to. And I could repeat that, and then set up another, and another, and another, all very fast.

...And then give them up just as fast when they don't work out – and that's the problem.

It's called "barrier to entry", and it refers to the difficulties in getting into a business. When the effort or cost to do something is low (as we discussed earlier with Internet products), that barrier is low, and easy to get over. And although people don't talk about it, the barrier goes both ways: If it's easy to start a site, it's just as easy to leave it off. This is especially a problem online, because so many ideas look great at first; but once started, the next idea always looks better and more profitable (and easier than the current one). So without persistence, it's very easy to grab the next project or idea that comes along.

For example, I've belonged to many online marketing communities over the years, and it seems every month there's a new idea: Affiliate sales, content sites, promote your book, become a 'guru' on a topic, and so on. The person who built an affiliate site last month is encouraged to try selling a book this month, or go in yet another direction. The result is that old projects are abandoned, or at least not given enough attention.

For that reason, when you are planning your website, give some thought as to how you're going to continue with it. For example:

• How much time and effort will you need to make a success of this business? Are you prepared to invest that time?

• What if you get busy elsewhere? How much effort will the site require to keep going at a minimum?

• When the "going gets tough", is this a project that will keep you motivated and working on it?

• What is the end game for this site? Just as you have goals for success, have you thought about failure, and at what point you should move on?

These are questions worth asking before you start a site, because it's important to realize that a website is an investment, not just of money, but in your time and energy; those are things you can't get back, so it's worth considering in advance.

And, while a book like this can make it quick going, you'll still spend a lot of time with your website in the future. Pick wisely, plan to follow through, and it will be a worthwhile investment you will be delighted with.

Do It Yourself? Hire Someone? Here's What You Need To Get Started

A website online is a funny place. It doesn't really exist; it's just made of bits of energy on a transmission line, or magnetic patterns on a hard drive somewhere "out there". Yet it is every bit as real as a local business. Plus it requires as much setup and planning as any business. And of course, it can be screwed up just like any other business if it's not done right.

So, let's do your website right!

Websites are like houses: Pretty, but a lot goes on behind the scenes. No matter what site you end up creating for yourself, you'll need the same basic essentials. That's fortunate, since once you've learned how to build a website using WordPress, you're well on your way to building any website using WordPress.

To set up your site you'll need the following:

• A domain name.

• A place for your domain (called web hosting, or just hosting), where the actual site will be erected.

• The site framework itself (built, as you might have guessed, using WordPress).

• A look or style to go with that framework (that's our WordPress Theme).

• Content, since no site is worthwhile without something to look at once you get there.

So to begin, let's spend a moment on the site itself, starting with the domain name.

A Domain Name To Call Your Own

Picking a domain name, a good domain name, is not a simple matter. Unless you already have a domain name (say, a company name or product name), then coming up with a brand new one will be a major endeavor. That's as it should be – it's effectively your brand name, calling card, and 'home' on the Internet, all wrapped up in one name, and so worth spending some time on.

Unfortunately, many people have over the years grabbed up domains and 'sat' on them, not using them, but preventing others from using them, too. Called cybersquatting, it's a very real problem, and there's not much you can do unless the domain infringes on a trademark. The result is that simple combinations of familiar words are likely not available, unless you want to pay a premium to buy them.

> Buying a current domain name from a cybersquatter is not trivial. In my experience, don't even consider this route unless several thousand dollars for a domain name interests you! As well, use a reputable service to handle the transaction (such as Escrow.com to manage payment). In contrast, with just a bit of mental brainstorming, you can probably come up with a name that you'll like just as well, and at a huge savings!

To pick a good, inexpensive domain name today, then, you'll need to be creative:

• The easiest way I've found to come up with a new name is to go online with a thesaurus, and look up similar words to those you are interested in, as they occur to you.

• While single word domains are not available, obscure terms can be. For instance, old Latin or Greek words might still be available, or technical terms. Of course, an obscure word might mean you'll need to constantly explain it to visitors.

• Joined words have possibilities. After all, 'word' + 'press' made a domain that is easy to read, spell, and understand; even without knowing the product, you have a rough idea what a WordPress must do. While pairings of common words are less likely now (thank those cybersquatters again), triplets or quadruplets may still work.

• Likewise, longer phrases can still be found. For my wife's book website, her protagonist was a Plant Lady (Horticultural Technician to be exact, but "plant lady" was easier to spell). Unfortunately, all plant lady name variations were taken

---

(PlantLady.com, ThePlantLady.com, etc.) So we went for PlantLadyMysteries.com instead, which was perfect, since the novels were (and would remain) mystery–oriented.

• Another important point: If the domain is going to be about you, try to get your name as a domain. Authors especially should do this. Consider first name + last name. If that isn't available, try adding middle initials, or variations of the first name (For example, I could try variations added to 'pankhurst.com' like 'davidpankhurst.com'; or 'dave', 'davem', 'davidm', 'd', or even 'dm') And so on. If that's still an issue, you might even add 'author' in front for writer sites. You could even use dashes if absolutely necessary, since branding of your name is so important, but only as a last resort.

• I use domain names ending in .com for my sites. But should you stay with .com, or explore .org, .net, .biz and the other types of domain extensions (called TLD, or top level domains)? In a nutshell, no. People are used to adding .com to the end, and if the .com name is not available, taking an alternative TLD is not a good idea – people might type in the .com by accident, and you'll send your hard–won traffic to another website. There are a few exceptions: Using country codes for specific local sites (like a .ca domain for a business located in Canada, or .co.uk for Britain), or .org if you're starting a non–profit organization. But even in these cases, I still recommend you spend some time getting a .com version of the same name. You might never make the .com version your main site, but by owning it, you can send traffic that accidentally goes there back to your main site, capturing those errant visitors.

• What about odd wordings? For a while, 'z' was popular as a substitute for 's' (wordz, brainz, ideaz, etc.) Slang, jargon, and technical terms can all provide alternative domains. The question is, will your target audience "get it"? If not, or you have to explain it to everyone you meet, then you have an uphill battle.

• Spelling is also an issue. If words are hard to spell, then they are hard to say – and people will have problems with them. National variations can also be an issue: In the United States, the words gray, analyze and favor are spelled grey, analyse and favour in Britain. Use one or the other, and you immediately subdivide your visitors, and risk sending traffic to someone else using the 'other' spelling. Instead, try to find words that are easy to say and spell in any country (again, WordPress.com is a great example).

• Dashes or no dashes? In the past, dashes separated words, and made it easier for search engines to figure out what you meant. However, dashes are a real distraction to humans using your site, and harder to type in (not to mention trying to say the domain to someone over the phone!) Often, they will forget, and end up somewhere else. Computers are getting smarter, but you shouldn't expect people to, so I'd err on the side of not using them these days.

• With any domain pick, run it past others and get their views. A domain that sounds great to you may make others go 'huh'? That's a sure sign it's not a catchy as you were hoping for.

One final caution about domain names: Make plans to search for them and grab them at the same time. I have had several occasions in the past where I've looked at potential domains, debated whether to get them or not, and waited a few days. When I tried to get them later, they were taken. While it's possible more than one person came up with a domain idea at almost the same time, there have been reports of sites that monitor domain lookups, and grab some of the domains searched for themselves. Whether true or not, I've had domain picks disappear too often to recommend "sleeping on it" when you have a great domain idea. Decide and grab it as soon as possible.

And if you find one you love, don't hesitate to grab variations as well immediately, including the .net, .org, and regional ones of the country you live in, such as .us for the United States and .ca for Canada. You might also consider ones with 's' at the end of words, common misspellings, or dashes in between words. It's a small price to pay in advance, and you can always release extra domain names in the future if you don't need them. Called "letting them expire", it simply means not renewing them in a year's time.

Finally, where to get domain names? While everyone has a preferred location, I've used GoDaddy.com and Namecheap.com for years without problems. Both are very inexpensive. I tend to use GoDaddy for the lower cost names, and you can often find online coupon codes to save even more; however, Namecheap offers inexpensive domain name protection. This works by hiding the ownership of the domain, which can be helpful if you wish to keep your domain's contact information private (by default, your domain contact information can be easily looked up online).

On Being The Perfect Host

Hosting is the term for the actual website location you place your content on. Every

---

website out there ultimately is on a storage drive, much like the one in your home computer. In fact, your home computer is very similar to the machines that host everyone's websites around the world, although your connection to the Internet is far too slow to make your own "home computer website" practical.

As you can imagine, if all you need is a computer and Internet connectivity (and software, but much of that, like WordPress, is free), then just about anyone and everyone is willing to offer hosting. But the fact is, there are big names out there that are very good, very reliable, and very cheap. So despite that bargain on eBay or the 'special' that your local guy told you about (don't laugh, that's how some of my earlier websites started out), the fact is, the larger sites are the way to go. Ask trusted sources for recommendations: Ones I've tried and used in the past include HostGator.com and GoDaddy.com hosting. Another I've also heard good things about (but not tried personally) is 1and1.com

These companies offer a variety of plans, with different sizes, capacities, and services. For that reason, you'll need to check a few things for any hosting plan you consider getting, specifically:

• It's very easy to see what others say about a site by searching online. Of course, companies are wise to that, so not all information out there is reliable. For example, most companies have an affiliate program, meaning that a link on a review can mean money for the reviewer – not the best way to provide a completely unbiased report! Nonetheless, with a bit of digging, you can often find out what most people honestly say about a company.

• Likewise, pay attention to whatever complaints there are. The Internet makes it very easy to complain, and people do. So you will find bad experiences. See if their problem could be your problem; for example, if their complaint was ignored for a week, there's a real possibility that could happen to you! And of course, if there are a lot of complaints, that could be a sign of a general problem with the company. But to be fair, any large company will have complaints, so you'll have to decide if the proportion is reasonable or not.

• Look for recommendations. People tend to stay with hosting they like, and that is a pretty good recommendation in itself. As you meet people, don't be afraid to ask what hosting they use, and ask them why in particular – not only will you get concrete reasons, you'll also learn more about hosting.

It's a pain to move to a different host. In fact, it compares a lot to moving to a new house, since everything has to uprooted and moved, things won't work afterward, you'll need to refurnish a bit, etc. For that reason, it pays to spend time beforehand, to make sure you don't regret the host you end up using.

However, hosting in itself is not the only issue. You also need to pick the configuration for your website. For example, at the low end of the hosting platform is virtual hosting, where dozens, even hundreds, of sites share a server computer and a hard drive or two. For small, unpopular (that is, with low amounts of visitor traffic) sites this can be ideal, since costs stay low, and the capacity is enough for those kinds of websites. For about $10 a month, you can set up several websites and give them all a nice home – perfect for starting out.

A variation of this is sometimes called a Reseller Plan. You still share your computer resources with other people's sites, but you have the added benefit of setting up separate 'fiefdoms' of your own, groups of websites that are independent and can't interfere with each other. This is in contrast with the virtual plans, where all your websites are on the same actual hard drive location, and so can 'talk' to each other if you wish. The advantage of this is that for just a little more money you can set up websites that are completely unrelated to you, for example if you wish to create websites to sell. Because hosting plans like this give you more options for your websites, they tend to be better in the long run than a single–user virtual hosting plan.

However, for both of these plans, you still share a computer with other users. This can be a drain on resources, and so a way to avoid that is a virtual dedicated hosting plan, where you still share a computer, but each one of you has a completely independent 'virtual' computer (actually, a software program that pretends to be a separate computer, and does it very well). One benefit is enhanced security, since you are running an independent server program with no connection to your neighbors whatsoever. Also, you get improved performance: Unlike the other hosting plans we've discussed, you usually share the physical computer with a very small number of other users, typically under a dozen (as compared to possibly hundreds on other plans). The downside of this? Usually it requires more technical knowledge to use. Unless you have access to a web hosting support person (such as an employee in your company), these have the potential to become maintenance headaches.

Sharing with a lot of people, sharing with a few people: Obviously, the ultimate here is sharing with no people at all. And that option is called self hosted or dedicated hosting, where you actually rent a whole server for your own use. While more expensive, and more labor intensive to maintain, this is the ultimate in power; a whole computer hooked up to the Internet, with no one else hogging the controls! However, like virtual dedicated hosting, you do more of the work yourself. As well, this capacity is overkill for most people, and means you're spending more money than you need to, often 10 to 40 times more than a minimal hosting plan. But for sites anticipating high traffic volume, these can be great systems to use.

If you do need one, try to find a Managed Server Plan, where the staff takes care of software updates. Otherwise, you will have to do the software updating, or 'patching', of the server's software yourself. This can get very labor intensive and prone to mistakes, yet is an absolute necessity to prevent security issues (hackers never sleep, and they love to find unpatched servers).

With all these options, it can be hard to make a decision right away. However, for most people, the best compromise is the reseller account, since it makes it easier to set up sites, but gives you some room to grow. Less than that, and you might feel cramped and limited in a year or two; more than that, and you might find a lot of your time is spent getting to know your server, whether you want to or not! Of course, if you have someone technical ready to help out, take their suggestions and recommendations into account, since they will be managing the site for you.

By the way, you'll notice in all these plans I never discussed specifics: Bandwidth (how much your site can transmit over the Internet, such as web pages), website space (how much room you have on your "hard drive"), number of email accounts, what services are available, etc. The reason is simple: WordPress can get along with very little, far less than what even the smallest website plan offers nowadays. In fact, many sites offer to install WordPress as part of their package – proof they have enough room!

And as for email, with the power of free services like Gmail, you may not even use your site's email system. But if you do use it, the plans out there provide plenty of capacity for a WordPress–run site.

However, there is one area you might want to pay attention to – the control panel. This program handles the actual nuts and bolts of your site, and it's where you'll go to set up email accounts, activate domain names, manage your website and databases, and more. The most popular one out there is a program called cPanel, and if you have a choice, pick it. The reason is that its popularity means it is well documented. If you need to understand something, a search on any topic with "how to ... cPanel" should give you plenty of results. Of course, if you are familiar with a competing product, then go ahead and use it. But if in doubt, I've found cPanel a good choice for my sites; and for those ones where I've used another control panel, I've always wished for cPanel!

By now, your head must be spinning with all these new terms, and the technology needed to run your website. If that's the case, perhaps the best thing to do is to offload the technical work, and call in a professional.

The Pros And Cons Of Hiring Pros (And Not Cons)

The Time of the Generalist is over. You have your strengths. In fact, you're putting a website on the Internet to feature what you are very good at. So doesn't it make sense to get someone who's very good at what they do to take care of the details of your site?

In fact, unless you are short of money, or want the experience (for instance, your business involves website management in some way), then you likely can spend your time elsewhere much more profitably. Website maintenance is not for everyone, and hiring the person who enjoys doing it, and doing it well, will free you up to concentrate on your core business.

What then should you look for in a 'tech' person?

I could go on about the various online business sites (such as Upwork.com, Freelancer.com, or Fivrr.com) where you can hire someone to help, but the fact of the matter is, in most any fair–sized town there's someone who can help you. As well, friends and acquaintances can likely recommend a 'go–to' guy or gal to help you, someone they can vouch for. Local can be valuable, especially in the beginning, because unless you understand tech, a nearby 'hand' to hold on to is worthwhile, as the minutiae of website management can be daunting.

Take for instance setting up your domain name. It's actually very easy to connect your domain name to your website. You change the directory entries for the domain (called the nameserver entries) to point to your website's nameservers, which were likely sent to you in an email when you signed up for your hosting plan. However, the actual procedure varies from company to company. And while the online person you hire should have no problems, you may have questions, and someone local you can call up right away when DNS propagation seems to fail is a lot easier than waiting for an email.

What's DNS propagation? The whole Internet rests on a system of using words to represent Internet addresses (which can look something like this: 192.168.100.3). Those numbers are hard to remember, and can change frequently, so someone came up with the idea of using an index of text names – domain names – and the Internet Protocol, or IP, addresses they point to (think Really Huge Old Fashioned Paper Phone Book and you have the idea). Those entries are called Domain Name System entries, or DNS for short.

One advantage with using the DNS is that you can move your domain with a quick change of the DNS entry, and point it to a new IP address. It's somewhat like keeping your phone number when you move. However, like a phone book, it takes a while for everyone to get notified about your new address. And while the new phone book may be a year away, the changeover online, or DNS propagation, is usually completed in 48 hours, often much less.

Bottom line: If you're already comfortable working with people online, feel free to go out and hire online; otherwise, find someone local you can trust. If no one comes to mind, just ask around. Like a good mechanic, people will know of a good tech person if they do work online.

Some other things to keep in mind:

• Trust is important, so follow your gut. This person will be entrusted with your domain name and hosting passwords at a minimum, so you have to be feel good about them.

• A professional will have a portfolio of work they've done, as well as references you can contact. Check them out, even phoning a reference or two. If not, consider whether you can work together or not.

• Don't be afraid to use a company. You'll likely spend more, but a full service company will also save you in other ways. Time, for instance; after all, they can probably split jobs between two or more employees, speeding things up.

If your time is valuable, hiring someone can let you focus your time and energies elsewhere. But of course you may prefer to save your cash. The good news is that if you wish to do it yourself, there are many tools that make setting up and configuring

WordPress very easy for a beginner, and of course anyone else for that matter.

For those hardy ones of you, we'll discuss those tools in a moment; but for everyone, let's look at the final goal, by taking WordPress itself out for a spin.

Working With Your New WordPress Blog

Using WordPress to its fullest extent can fill a book (and has) – but many of the features are unnecessary for day to day use. Basically, you need to do some things once (like setting up your blog), and some things day after day (like writing articles). There's also maintenance, which for WordPress usually means little more than checking for new versions (done automatically for you), and upgrading plugins as needed.

The next trick goes into the nuts and bolts of that first item, setting up your blog – all that one–time stuff you may want to pass on to someone else – but first, let's see how those daily tasks are managed by visiting a WordPress blog.

The first step is to log in. For security, all the "interesting bits" of the blog are locked away in the Administration section. You can get to it via a link on the front page of the blog (usually on the sidebar near the bottom) labeled 'Login' or 'Admin'. If it's not there, you can type in the URL directly. Just use the blog's home URL and add /wp-admin/ to it. If for example my blog was at egwebsite.com then this would take me to the Admin login form:

```
http://egwebsite.com/wp-admin/
```

At this point, you log in with the password and login name given to you by your installer (or when you set it up yourself). Useful tip: Bookmark this destination page once you're inside (called the dashboard), and you won't have to go through as much effort logging into WordPress in the future.

Now you've made it inside, here's the other task you'll need to know: Writing.

With a fully set up blog, the main job now is adding your words to it. Writing articles, or 'content' creation (a somewhat insulting generic term for writing, somewhat like "processed meat" is for whatever goes into hot dogs!), is a matter of doing the following steps:

• Clicking on the left side menu where it says **Posts**.

• Clicking on the newly shown submenu item ADD NEW.

• The page that now appears is for adding posts. Enter the title in the topmost line (click on the entry "Enter title here" to make it go away, and start typing), then the article in the box below that section, and click on the button at the right marked SAVE DRAFT to save it, but not show it to the world.

• Edit, tweak, adjust or what have you. When you're done, click on the PUBLISH button to send the post out into the world.

> In WordPress, the options on the left side are the way to navigate throughout the Administration section. Called menus, most entries have 'children' entries below, called submenus. For instance, the steps to create an article involve clicking on the POSTS menu entry, then the ADD NEW submenu entry, or to shorten it, POSTS; ADD NEW. We'll use this shorter form from now on. For example, to create a new Page instead of a Post, we'd click on the PAGES; ADD NEW submenu, which means clicking first on PAGES, then clicking on ADD NEW.

Of course, it's possible to complicate this, as all software seems to enjoy doing. In fact, you will more than likely do the following as well:

• Select the proper editor to write in. WordPress has two editors here. One is used by clicking on the VISUAL tab above the edit box, near the right corner, and displays the text fully formatted, including things like underlining and bolding. The other, clicked on with the TEXT tab above the edit window, is a text editor; in this one, bold and underline are known by their HTML codes. So the same sentence can look different in each editor:

Visual Editor:

```
The Visual editor displays formatting like italics and underline; the HTML
    editor shows the codes.
```

Text Editor:

```
The Visual editor displays formatting like <i>italics</i> and
    <u>underline</u>; the Text editor shows the codes.
```

Try it – type text in one and then switch to the other to look at the result.

And while either editor in WordPress will do the job, it's a good idea to pick one and consistently use it, otherwise, switching back and forth will get confusing. I prefer the Text editor because I like entering HTML codes directly, but that's just me.

• Paste or write the article. You can write directly into the WordPress edit box and create a finished post. Many do, and sometimes I do as well. But I have better tools on my own computer, so I prefer to use the more powerful Word Processor there, and then copy and paste it into the editor box. One advantage: You have a backup of the articles on your computer automatically.

• Save it. Save the article now; in fact plan to save it many times. The button marked SAVE DRAFT (at the right side) takes care of that.

• Decide when and how to publish it. When you hit the PUBLISH button, the current time is used for the article date. For blog posts that's usually fine, but you can easily change it. Say you've written five articles, and you'd rather they appear each day, instead of all at once. You can adjust each article's time and date by clicking on the EDIT link beside the entry "Publish immediately" at the right of the page; when clicked, it opens to a calendar entry form you can use to enter the date for publishing. Remember to click on **OK** after to set it, and of course, you'll need to save the article again.

• Publish it. Remember to click on PUBLISH to finish off. Now WordPress will use the publish date you set (which by the way is based on your blog's time settings, which are found in the Admin SETTINGS; GENERAL submenu), and makes that article available to the world at approximately that day and time. Also at that time, it will do the announcing to the world of the article via pings, hopefully bringing search engine traffic shortly.

• Tweak some more. If you're like me, the final article is still not perfect, and you'll want to adjust a bit. Notice that the SAVE DRAFT button disappeared once you published your post, and in its place is UPDATE. Just edit and click on that to save the changes to your now–live article.

That's the basics – if you can successfully write a post and publish it, then you have the skills to run your own blog. Of course, many people like to do a bit more, and tinkering is very easy with WordPress. So in preparation for the next chapter, let's look at some of the tools you can use to get more out of WordPress.

File Transfer Protocol

One valuable tool is for FTP. FTP, or File Transfer Protocol, is the way your computer talks directly to your website to move files back and forth. Unlike the way web browsers work, FTP goes both directions (called uploading and downloading files) to and from the website. It also has complete access to your site, allowing you to put files anywhere, even places a website browser can never 'see'.

If you've moved files around on your computer with a tool like Windows Explorer, you know how file transfer programs work. You just pick up a file (click and drag) and drop it in another location. With an FTP program, that location can be "out there" on the Internet, like your website.

For programs like WordPress, there are many little files that comprise the whole program, and placing them on the website is an ideal use for an FTP program.

Note that FTP is less necessary than it was at one time. For example, most web hosts have a simple 'one-click' style WordPress install, and you won't have to upload the program files and tweak to get started. However, understanding FTP can be helpful in case you want to put a file on your website from time to time.

If you plan to set up your own blog and change files from time to time, you'll need a good FTP tool to handle it easily (strictly speaking, cPanel and other web host programs do provide FTP support, but for serious work they will soon drive you crazy). My favorite is the free program FileZilla, found at

```
http://filezilla-project.org/
```

We'll explain how to use it in the chapter on plugins; however, you can also search online on "tutorial filezilla" for more information.

Besides moving files onto your website, you'll likely want to change them – and that brings up text editors, in two 'flavors'.

Handy Tools For Writing

As I mentioned, I prefer to write my articles on my computer, and then copy and paste them into WordPress. Besides giving me a backup copy, it allows me to do a better job of writing, since my computer's word processor includes more features and tools.

My favorite? Although I own Microsoft Word, I prefer to use Open Office, or its more recent update, Libre Office, which are available at

```
http://www.openoffice.org/
http://www.libreoffice.org/
```

They include a full word processor, spreadsheet, database tool, and graphic tool, all for the great price of – free. While only the word processor is needed for WordPress, the other tools will soon become useful for much of the work related to your website (for example, the spreadsheet can help track numbers of visitors, or advertising expenses and results).

Another feature of Open Office I like: It's extremely easy to output text as a PDF file (the menu option FILE; EXPORT AS **PDF** does the trick). This format, short for Portable Document Format, means that you can create a report that is easily read on many computers. As I've already explained regarding my whitepapers, PDF provides a way to turn your words into money–making guides, fast. Even if you don't sell them, writing and giving away a report on a technical subject can be a great way to promote your site.

Of course, my suggestion of Open Office assumes you don't already have a favorite word processor. If so, as long as you're happy with the results, then there's no need to change. However, if you'd like to try something new, or want a more powerful package of business software to work with, then give Open Office a try.

Now, similar to Word Processing, yet different, is Text Editing. The difference?

• Text editing is used for computer text, whereas word processing is for readable text (although to be fair, both can be used for either purpose if you're careful).

• Word processors like to tweak, and computer code cannot allow that. Load in any of the PHP code files WordPress uses into a word processor (plugins, widgets and themes), and the result will likely be broken if you tried to save it and use it. The reason is that computers are less tolerant of text differences than we are.

For example, all quotes look pretty reasonable when you read them, but that's not good enough for computer software, which likes only one of these:

" " "

Dashes are another problem. Where we might have no trouble with these:

- - —

A program might complain about two of these three (the last two), and when a program complains, it break down – like WordPress.

• We read (and think) in paragraphs, and word processors think that way too. However, text editors think in lines, and a line can be very long without wrapping around to the next line (each of these book paragraphs would appear in a text editor as long, long lines stretching to the right). While vital for organizing computer code, it's annoying to work with for people. For these and other reasons, word processors do a poor job of editing computer text.

Instead, use a text editor. My favorites? The free (and Open Source) Notepad++, found at

```
https://notepad-plus-plus.org/
```

or the free psPad, found at

```
http://www.pspad.com/
```

Both let you load and save text files, and make it easy to edit them. Either one is fine for the task. A note for advanced users: Of the two, I find psPad to be better when using Regular Expressions, and Notepad++ for function/code collapsing.

Using an editor is almost the same as a word processor. And using it on files from your website is only a bit harder, as we'll look at now.

Editing Your Files

WordPress is calling: You've decided you need to fix a file, adjust a theme, or tweak a plugin on your website. So what do you do?

You can edit files online, since WordPress has a built in text editor (besides its word processor for articles). However, this can cause huge problems if you're not extremely careful. Nonetheless, if you're in a bind, here's the steps:

• Log into Admin, and use the PLUGINS menu (if you are editing a plugin file) or the APPEARANCE menu (for editing theme files). In both cases, the EDITOR submenu will let you edit the files.

• For themes, a list of themes is displayed in a drop–down box at the right; select one to display that theme's files below, then click on any file entry in the list to display that one in the editor window. Edit it, and save via the UPDATE FILE button.

• Editing plugin files is similar: Select a plugin from the drop–down box, and then select to edit any file displayed, saving after.

As you can imagine, the reason this is dangerous is that in each case you are working directly with your only copy of a live blog file. If it gets messed up, or you delete too much, you have no immediate backup copy. Damage to the file online would mean that your whole blog is broken until you can fix the issue.

For that reason, like writing my articles on my computer first, I edit my computer files there, and I recommend you do as well. Basically, I follow these steps whenever possible:

• Download the file. Using an FTP program, I copy the file from my website to somewhere local on my computer.

• Make a copy. Even if I know the file is one I have a copy of, I like to make a copy immediately for consistency – it's amazing how many times I've skipped this step, and that turns out to be the file I only have one copy of (and then the file gets damaged, to boot). Murphy is not your friend, but he is the law, so placate him and make a copy.

• Load and edit it. Now I can use the local copy in my text editor, make my changes, and save.

• Upload the changes. Using the FTP program, I can place the file right back into the blog, and test it out. If there's a problem, I can use my backup copy to restore things to normal. And if it needs more changes? All I have to do is repeat: Make more editor changes, save, and upload until it's finished.

Following these steps, editing can be safe, and you've always got a fallback position if any file gets damaged.

By the way, this is an abbreviated outline of how I actually do things. In fact, I not only download the single file I'm going to work on, but whatever group it's a part of – plugin package, widget files, theme files – and make a backup copy of them all. That way, I have a complete copy of the object, and I keep all the relevant files together (good if I make lots of changes). However, when you're just beginning, that may be too much work. But at a minimum, make a local copy of the current file.

More Tools And Techniques Online

FTP and editing files are two of the main tasks you'll want to know if you work online with your WordPress blog. Whether you do it yourself or get someone to do the work for you, you'll find that these techniques will be useful again and again, even if only to understand what others are doing (or what you're paying for!)

Part of what makes WordPress great is the huge storehouse of information online. Type a search on 'WordPress', combined with another topic, and you will likely find many articles and videos explaining the specific technique you're interested in. And if not, there are many forums where you can ask questions, including what I like to call "WordPress Central" and the WordPress Forum, found at

```
https://wordpress.org/support/
```

Now with an understanding of the basics of using WordPress, and the tools to work with it, let's move on to the next section – how to make the foundation of your blog rock–solid for your future business.

Set Up WordPress Properly Now So You Won't Have Regrets Later

What is it about trailer parks that tornadoes always seem to go there?

I was watching the news today, when yet another trailer park was hit and leveled. It's practically a cliche that trailer homes are like tornado magnets.

However, the answer is much simpler. If a house with a concrete foundation is hit by a tornado, and a trailer home on loose cinder blocks is hit, which one do you think will look worse when the television cameras arrive?

It's a fact: A good foundation makes a huge difference.

And that's why this chapter is the single most important one you'll read in this book.

Because if you don't have a solid foundation for your WordPress blog, you'll be kicking yourself as long as you have it!

Where Is My Site, Dude?

Take for example where exactly you place your blog on your website. WordPress is flexible about this, and you can even move your blog from spot to spot around your site if you really wish. However, the Internet is not so forgiving, and once it gets used to a specific web page of content at a specific place – the URL of that page – it doesn't like to change (and more importantly, if people link to your site, they don't want to change, either). Like moving to a new house, it can be done, but it's not simple or easy (if you feel it's necessary, do a search on "301 redirects" for how to do it right). However, you can avoid the hassle completely by setting up your blog in the proper place the first time.

URLs on the Internet correspond to files on a hard drive, the hard drive containing your website. For instance, depending on your point of view, these are the same location:

```
http://egwebsite.com/myblog/index.php
/users/~egweb/html_docs/myblog/index.php
http://egwebsite.com/myblog/
```

The first one is a URL to a file (in this case, the root file of my imaginary blog). The second is the same file, but the path on the hard drive that actually stores the file (if this was Windows, the path might start with C:\ or D:\, but in Unix type servers it's a bit different).

The third one is a bit confusing – it's actually the same URL as the first, but without the index.php at the end. By default, most web servers go ahead and assume index.php if no file name is provided at the end of the URL (they'll also optionally try index.htm and index.html). Thus, it does refer to the same file, but implied.

By the way, to round this out, here's the components of the URL: The root is the location, at egwebsite.com, the /myblog/ is the subdirectory 'off' of the root directory, and index.php is the file found there.

With those things in mind then, where is the best place for your blog? You have two choices – the site root or a subdirectory:

• The site root. Placing your files at the top of the site means the blog is the first thing people see when they visit. So in that case, the blog IS the site; the front page of the blog is the front page of the site, and moving around the site is moving around the blog. The advantage is your site is set up as soon as your blog is live, with nothing else to do. However, if you plan to install any other software on your site (for example, a help desk program or forum), the files can conflict, since usually they can't both be in the website root directory at the same time. For example, most programs have a generic file called index.php, and there obviously can only be one at a time in any given location. For cases like that, the other program will need to be placed in a subdirectory.

• Another directory (that is, a subdirectory, like our example with /myblog/). The pros and cons are almost exactly reversed from the previous option for the root. A blog here can coexist with other programs easily, since they are in other directories. However, since the blog is not the root, visitors will have to see something else when they drop in, unless they somehow go directly to the blog's directory. The directory option is ideal if you are adding a blog to an older site, since you can add a brand new subdirectory, and place the blog there.

As a general recommendation, since WordPress blogs are so useful, you should place your blog in the root directory of a new site. Likewise, to avoid installation hassles, place it in a subdirectory of an old site. And if your site needs other add on features, like a forum or helpdesk, I recommend placing them in subdirectories as well.

As a further suggestion, if you do decide to place the blog in a subdirectory, avoid calling that directory /blog/. It may sound sensible, but you're wasting some valuable search engine potential here. How? Imagine your site is on dog training – which URL do you think a search engine will rank higher for dog information?

```
http://egwebsite.com/blog/
http://egwebsite.com/dog-training/
```

This trick alone won't send your site to the top of the listings, but all other things considered, a keyword–rich URL gives the search engines more to see – and more to rank on. Of course, if you want to be known for blog writing, then one of your main keywords will be 'blog', so feel free to use that as a directory. But even so, with people that search on the word 'blog', there's no harm in adding better focused keywords to the URL to fit:

```
http://egwebsite.com/dog-training-blog/
```

One caution however: Be careful of length. A long URL can be unwieldy, and since humans need to visit the site, you want to avoid overloading it with keywords here. After all, there's the individual article's URL portion to consider still, further adding to the length.

A few minutes spent determining the destination directory if you don't use the site root is worth the time, trust me: This is the 'foundation' your blog and site will rest on for a long, long time, so it pays to pick carefully, and wisely.

But once you have your location, it's time to do the deed and set up WordPress on your site. For this, you have two options, the easy(ish) or the hard(er) way.

The harder way is to configure the database; download, unpack, and upload the WordPress files yourself (via FTP); and then run through the install (which is a series of questions that appear when you open the blog's home page in your browser). It's the way I usually do it, and it has a few technical benefits – but none of those matter to you when starting out. So instead of explaining the hard way in any further detail, let's look at the easy way, and the ONLY way you're likely going to set up your blog, via cPanel and Fantastico.

Easy WordPress Setup With The Fantastic Fantastico

If you use cPanel for your web hosting plan, you may have noticed an icon called Fantastico. Fantastico comes with cPanel, and includes a simplified install system for popular programs, including WordPress. Using it, your WordPress blog can be up and running on your website in a few minutes, even if you've never done text editing or FTP before.

(A note: There are many installers out there, and Fantastico is just one of them. Check your web host for the installer they use, and follow their instructions for your site. However, the method here is similar across all installers.)

Here's the steps for Fantastico:

• From cPanel, click on the Fantastico logo icon to begin. You'll go to the Fantastico main panel.

• From Fantastico, click on 'WordPress' at the left side to begin.

• On the right the WordPress details will appear. Click on NEW INSTALLATION to start. Now you'll need to enter a few things at this point.

• The first item is the location for the blog (both the domain from a drop–down box at the top, followed by a subdirectory if you are using one). This will be the physical location of your blog, and should ideally be empty (since WordPress will crowd out anything there).

• Below that, you enter your login information. Unless you have reasons to change it, just use 'admin' (all lowercase) for the login name, and then an alphanumeric password of around 8–15 characters long (be careful to note your password somewhere). I recommend alphanumeric characters (that is, A to Z, a to z, and 0 to 9) because unusual characters have the possibility of not working right (for example, some foreign language letters). Alphanumeric characters provide plenty of combinations for secure passwords.

• The BASE CONFIGURATION section is where you enter the remaining fields to begin your install: ADMIN NICKNAME (your 'visible' name as it will appear on posts, such as

'Admin', or your real name), your EMAIL ADDRESS for maintaining the blog (where messages to you will be sent); the SITE NAME (blog name), and the DESCRIPTION (blog subtitle). These four entries can all be changed later on, by the way, so if you can't come up with the perfect blog title, just wing it for now.

• When all is filled in, click on INSTALL WORDPRESS to begin. The next panel will show your settings, and let you confirm everything. Click to continue, and poof – the install is done for you. At that point, you can visit your new blog and log in, using your Admin login (not your nickname) and password.

• One last step: Fantastico can be out of sync with the latest version. If so, once you've logged into the Admin section of WordPress you'll see a yellow bar across the top of each web page, asking you to upgrade. Go ahead by clicking on that link, and then select the UPDATE AUTOMATICALLY button on the next page.

That's it – with practice, it's likely you'll have a finished blog ready in under five minutes (and probably far less than that). And it's much easier than the old manual install!

Now that your website is up and running, it's time for the special tweaks to improve your blog.

Permalinks – The Single Biggest Boost To SEO!

Earlier, I explained about subdirectories, and how keywords in their name can make a difference for your blog installation. WordPress has another area for keywords that is absolutely vital, called permalinks.

Every article you create on your website ends up as an individual URL – a URL that the search engine can index.

By default an article might look like this:

```
http://egwebsite.com/?p=23
```

The `?p=23` refers to a post, and so this is a link to post number 23. What is article number 23, and why should search engines care? We don't know, and they don't care. But with permalinks, you can add keywords to that post's URL that they DO care about:

```
http://egwebsite.com/dog-training-dos-and-donts/
```

Now the article URL gives a clue about itself.

By the way, the article text part

```
dog-training-dos-and-donts
```

Is sometimes called a **slug**, so if you see a reference to slugs in a blog, it's probably referring to the text version of a link to a post, or page, or just about anything WordPress generates, such as author pages or category listings.

The technical details of permalinks are somewhat complex, but in a nutshell, a file called .htaccess on Apache servers creates what are called Rewrite Rules, internal rules that take that pretty URL here and changes it transparently into the ?p=23 that WordPress ultimately needs to do its job. So both WordPress and the search engines get what they want: WordPress, the necessary reference to its article, and search engines, a URL that includes key words, words that will help them target the web page in their search engine indexes.

WordPress has a template that specifies how the permalink is created – a little of this, a little of that – all molded into the final URL for any article. If you go to the SETTINGS; PERMALINKS submenu in Admin, you'll see where the permalink template entry is put in, and some of the possible parameters for them. For example, %postname% is replaced with the final article text link (also known as the post slug, or just slug). In our earlier example, the template for

```
http://egwebsite.com/dog-training-dos-and-donts/
```

Would look like this:

```
/%postname%/
```

The domain provides the first part, and /dog-training-dos-and-donts/ is the URL part for the article itself.

> By the way, I mention Apache, a free server that runs on Linux and other Unix style systems, but it isn't the only option out there. Windows offers a server program, and there are other types of server programs for other operating systems. However for WordPress I <u>strongly</u> encourage you to use an Apache system on a Unix style server, since each version of WordPress comes out well tested for it. I've had some nasty surprises in the past on Windows servers, and I find many of my troubleshooting problems for clients revolve around non–Apache web servers. So save yourself time and headaches – go with Apache!

Setting up a permalink is simplicity itself:

• Go to the **SETTINGS; PERMALINKS** submenu in Admin.

• Check on **CUSTOM STRUCTURE** to select it.

• Enter the appropriate permalink template text in the box beside it.

• Click on **SAVE CHANGES** to save it.

• To double–check, go to your main blog (home) page and reload it into your browser. Then click any post link – it should now be a nice URL, without the `?p=` stuff (if not, you may have an `.htaccess` issue or a server problem, which will require some tech help).

Notice I left out what the "appropriate permalink template text" in the permalink should be? What exactly to put in that entry for your permalinks is a popular question. It can also be a tough question, because permalinks are "carved in stone". You really want to set them up once and never change them, since the resulting URLs are needed by the search engines for indexing (and remember how I said search engines hate it when URLs change). Once a person changes their phone number, the old phone book is useless for them. Same thing for a permalink change – search engines can lose touch with the web pages. Although it's possible to redirect them, you're best to avoid that pain, so choose the permalink once, and choose it wisely.

For years I've suggested the `/%post_id%/%postname%/` code, which is first the blog ID (what the number in the `?p=` referred to in the original example URL) followed by that valuable article title 'slug'. However, this creates a problem if you ever move your blog, since migrating the article to the new site may change the blog ID (WordPress provides import and export options to make this transfer easy, but it can affect the ID). Changed ID means changed URL and unhappy search engines, if you use this permalink code.

An alternative is to leave off the ID. However, WordPress recommends not using the `/%postname%/` by itself for performance reasons, so I instead recommend a keyword style permalink.

Going back to dog–training, here's an entry that will get extra keywords into your blog's URL:

```
/dog-training/%postname%/
```

Which in our example would look something like this:

```
http://egwebsite.com/dog-training/dog-training-dos-and-donts/
```

Just some cautions:

• Add dashes in between words, without spaces, and avoid any other punctuation.

• Also, the number of keywords listed here should be very small, since it will be repeated for every post and can make URLs quite long, as this example shows.

• Likewise, it should be generic (don't use `dog-training` if some of your pages will deal with feeding, for example; `dog` alone might be better, or `canine` if you think people search for it).

• If you've already placed your blog in a subdirectory on your website, then you have enough keywords in your URL, so something short and sweet will do.

• On sites where the blog focus is not too clear when you're setting up, one option is to use a more general word, like `info`:

```
/info/%postname%/
```

By the way, you'll notice this isn't the way some people suggest setting up a permalink. For example, they might prefer adding `.html` at the end like this:

```
/%postname%.html
```

And others say to leave off the last '/' like this:

```
/%postname%
```

The reason to do it the way I suggest is simple: WordPress can make a single article split itself across multiple pages, and multiple pages mean more pages for visitors to view and see ads on. But both of these methods interfere with that. Whether you plan to show ads or not right now, having it set up for the future is like putting a larger electrical panel in your new home: It gives you room to grow later without a costly retrofit.

Now with your permalink set up, each article can be keyword–targeted when you write it. As I mentioned, the custom permalink entry is filled in with the slug text for each article. That bit of information is found when you write your article, immediately under the title. Labeled **PERMALINK**, it appears after you save your article, and is shown just under the title. You can change it by clicking on the **EDIT** button beside the link. By default, it will try to use the title you enter, replacing spaces with dashes and changing text to lowercase, but you don't want the default behavior. Unlike the article title, which is for humans first, and search engines second, this entry is all about the search engines. So here's some tips on how to create effective permalink slugs for articles:

• Use keywords, and ONLY keywords: "How To Train Fido Not To Bite" is a catchy title, but search engines don't care about Fido (or even know that Fido is a dog – from their point of view, it could be a chair or a color of paint). Change it to keywords in your permalink to get maximum impact, like:

```
how-train-dog-no-bite
dog-training-not-bite
```

And so forth.

• Use synonyms. In that example, we switched 'Fido' for 'Dog', which makes search engine sense. But perhaps something else would be better, like puppy, canine, collie, or chihuahua? And maybe 'training' should be different: Teaching, educating, encouraging, etc. It depends on your market. A search engine can take a search for "dog training" and send people to your web page, if you have those words somewhere there (including the URL). But it gets a bit muddy when people search on "spaniel training": Do the search engines know to send them to your site if the word 'spaniel' is nowhere to be found? Search engines have a very narrow understanding of language, and so this can be a way to widen it with synonyms.

• Use misspellings. Few people look at the URL, and won't hold a misspelling against you if it appears there. But search engines will use it to get you indexed elsewhere. If you find a lot of people misspell 'training' for example, then a different permalink might get you seen by those folks:

```
dog-traning-not-bite
```

Follow tricks like these when you save and publish your articles, and your permalinks will give you an extra boost when you write – and that boost can help your search engine ratings.

Feed Them Right

While not as popular as they once were, for those that use them, feeds are a great attention–getting device for your website. People can load a text–only version of your blog pages, see what is new to them, and read everything quickly. It's perfect for busy people on the go.

However, those 'visitors' get your text and little else. So you have a decision to make: Give them the whole content of each article, or let them have only a teaser, and require them to get the rest at your site.

You should know that this was a hotly–debated topic (usually by people who want their feeds to be full and freely available):

• A teaser feed may annoy some readers that expect a full article.

• A full article via feed means they have little reason to visit your blog, and it's the blog visitors that see your ads, not RSS readers!

At one time, that issue was quite cut and dried. Now it's a bit blurred, since Google allows ads in feeds (called AdSense for Feeds), meaning you can make money from RSS readers who don't come to your website. However, you can generally make more money from a site visitor, such as by having them sign up to your email list, so "full feeds" isn't often a great idea for a business.

My personal preference is to give only a partial feed. I want visitors to my site, and prefer them to drop by and sign up to my email list. Likewise, I encourage you to chop your feed, with one exception: If your goal is to be known as a writer, anything you can do to get your writing out there is worth the effort. Since your writing is in effect your main 'advertisement', then getting it as widely spread as possible is the way to go. But for everyone else? Get them to your site with a partial feed.

Fortunately, unlike permalinks, this is not a permanent decision. You can start with a partial one now, and change it with a click later on. The option is found in the SETTINGS; READING submenu of Admin, the entry "For each article in a feed, show..." Check one or the other, and click on SAVE CHANGES.

Pings Away

Pinging, as we discussed earlier, lets the world know you're here. The ping list is the listing of all the sites that get notified automatically whenever an article of yours goes live. One would think that a big ping list would be more effective, and in the past, I've recommended a long ping list. To edit this, you simply add the list of ping URLs to the UPDATE SERVICES box in the SETTINGS; WRITING submenu, one URL per line.

But the fact of the matter is that adding more and more to a ping list is a matter of diminishing returns. Many large ping lists have small or inactive sites included, making it time consuming to contact, with little extra benefit. Plus, large lists usually require frequent pruning to get rid of the failed sites. In contrast, the default list built into WordPress does a good job of getting word out about your site, with no maintenance necessary, so unless you really feel the need to add to it, I recommend leaving it as is. However, if you desperately want to add to the list, you can always visit WordPress for more: There is a link above the UPDATE SERVICES box called, well, Update Services, which takes you to

```
https://codex.wordpress.org/Update_Services
```

for a larger list you can use.

And as we've discussed before, there are two kinds of pinging – pinging when YOU publish, which is a message sent out using this list, and pinging when others link to your article. It's unfortunate that WordPress used the same term for two different parts of its program, but that's the way it goes.

Better Categories

Another change right away for your new blog is the category names. Categories consist of three parts: The actual visible category name, the URL link (category slug), and the description, seen on many blogs if you hold the mouse over a category name. Each of these has search engine benefits, and are great ways to get extra keywords onto your site. Since many blog designs will display the category list on all web pages in the sidebar, this lets you add those extra keywords in a natural way, helping search engines figure out the main topic or subject of your site as a whole. It's so important in fact that if you have a theme that doesn't show the category list on every page, consider getting another one, since that extra keyword bonus is not one to pass up lightly.

For example, if your blog deals with dog issues, one category could be "Training", while another could be "Food Recipes". For "Training", you might want the category to look like that (or possibly "Dog Training", so the keyword 'dog' appears on the page again), and the same for the category slug, that is, training or dog-training, all lowercase, with dashes replacing spaces (that slug is used for the URL, pointing to a web page that lists all posts in a given category). Finally, the description text could be more keyword–rich and readable, such as "Ways to train your dog".

To set these entries up, you click on the POST; CATEGORIES submenu, and enter the information at the left side of the panel, with title, slug, and description in the appropriate boxes.

Combined, this gives you more keywords for your page, and helps search engines understand your blog is about dogs – or anything else you want to focus on!

And by the way, you can add and refine categories as you go. If right now you don't plan to offer dog food recipes, then include a category for it or not – it's up to you. Many WordPress themes will not show empty categories, so you can set them up in advance; and if your theme does show them, it's more keywords after all. As well, you can add or edit the category description later on if you wish; however, you should make sure the category slugs are set properly before you add any articles, as changes there will affect the URL of any category pages.

Commenting – On Or Off?

On most blogs, comments forms are visible, ready to allow people to add their own opinions...

...and I don't like them!

For the most part, the blogs I set up are not blogs at all: They are non–blog sites that use WordPress as a convenient manager of web pages. However, using WordPress means that by default my sites allow blog–style commenting, even if the content I put on there is definitely not comment–oriented. For example, if I use a site for business or product information, I really don't want people always weighing in on the subject!

WordPress allows you to manage commenting, using the following settings in the SETTINGS; DISCUSSION submenu:

• "E–mail me whenever / Anyone posts a comment." This sends an email to you when comments come in. You should turn this on.

• "Before a comment appears / Comment must be manually approved." Combined with the previous entry, checking this means you'll receive an email to approve each comment, and so prevents comments from automatically appearing on the blog.

• "Allow people to post comments on new articles." This setting helps prevent commenting if off; however, it should be changed before you publish articles, since any posts you make before you turn this off will still allow comments. In that case, you'll have to edit each of those posts manually to turn off commenting.

Of course, many themes out there anticipate comments being turned on, and may display something (such as a form) whether you allow comments or not. Editing a theme to delete the comments display is no easy task, and each theme is different. The good news? Every theme should at least display a "comments are closed" message, as long as you change the WordPress settings to turn them off. But if you want a theme that is completely comment–disabled, I recommend you find someone who can modify it for you (ideally the creator of the theme).

Fortunately, not every site needs commenting turned off. In that case, your theme and your WordPress setup are ready to handle comments from eager fans. Simply check "Allow people to post comments on new articles" to turn it back on. However, you'll still want to keep the other settings to prevent unauthorized posting. The reason I recommend these is that automatic spam machines can visit your blog and add comments, whether your form is there or not! Because of this, a blog that automatically publishes every comment it gets will quickly be inundated with spam. These settings at least will let you know that there is a comment, and can give you the option to approve or delete it before it appears, since a notification email is sent to your address after every comment received (via your email address, as set in the SETTINGS; GENERAL submenu).

Of course, these settings aren't perfect, and you'll still get some spam as soon as the world sees your blog – the liability of getting known! However, there is a solution for this; in the next chapter, we'll look at a great spam–killer plugin that every blog should use.

Still More Tweaks

To conclude this chapter, here's a list of other details you may want to adjust in WordPress once you're up and running, and why:

• Configure the SETTINGS; GENERAL panel. Check and confirm your blog title and tagline here, as well as your email address and time settings (and time zone). For example, WordPress starts the week on Monday, but I routinely change this to Sunday.

• While there, decide how your blog URL will appear, with or without the www. in front. Like any other URL change, you'll want to set it once and keep it that way from now on, so take a moment to decide (don't worry, either is fine). Edit both the WORDPRESS ADDRESS and SITE ADDRESS entries to match your choice and save.

• Select your theme, activate it, and configure. Once active, use the various submenus in the APPEARANCE menu to add/rearrange widgets, customize the logo or artwork if not already done, and edit any menus as needed for your posts.

Besides these items, you'll want to consider your website 'skeleton'. Articles (posts) will be written later. But right now you'll want some fixed web pages (pages) for various items:

(Note: Some of these web pages involve legal stuff. This is NOT a legal textbook, or legal advice; simply where to find further info on the Internet. If you are concerned about your legal standing on your blog, it is important you do the research, or even consider hiring legal advice.)

• About page. By default, WordPress adds this page, so now you can fill it out. Include anything appropriate for your site.

• Contacts. If you feel that others need to contact you, here is the place for that. You can include a contact form, or a link to another location, such as a help desk if you have it, or another site that manages contacts. The next chapter will show a contact form plugin that will do much of the setup work for you. One warning: If you instead decide to publish your email address here, make it hard for spammers to 'harvest' by leaving off the '@' symbol, and varying the text on the page:

```
myaddress (at) egwbsite.com
myaddress + egwbsite.com (replace the + with @)
```

• Legalese. Depending on your site use, you may wish to add legal information, such as disclaimers, licensing, etc. Especially for blogs that will discuss products for a fee (like a paid review site), you need to inform visitors that you do this. One easy solution in this case is to add a new page labeled "Disclosure Policy", and enter your details there. If you don't have anything yet, you can search online under 'disclosure policy generator', 'disclosure policy template', or 'disclosure policy example' for something you can adapt and use.

• Privacy policy. Likewise, sites need to explain what their privacy policy is and what is done with user data collected, especially for Europe, with the GDPR (General Data Protection Regulation). A search on 'privacy policy generator' or 'GDPR policy generator' should help.

• Permissions and copyright. You might want a page to explain what can be done with the content. This can be as permissive or restrictive as you want, of course. For example, some sites use a Creative Commons License, a very relaxed usage license, possibly in hopes of others borrowing content, and giving them wider exposure because of it. You can find out more about Creative Commons licensing from their site at:

```
http://creativecommons.org/
```

But whatever license you use, make sure people are aware of what they can and can't do with the content you place on your site.

In conclusion, your blog is set up, and configured with the basic settings to get you running. Now it's time to enhance your WordPress blog with those extra bits of goodness – plugins, widgets, and themes...

Attract Search Engines With Those Secret Weapons – Plugins And Widgets

When I was a kid, I dreamed of owning a locksmith shop (not one of my best dreams, I'll admit). I'd scan the advertisements in the back of Popular Science, and imagine having one of those machines that ground out keys. With a machine like that, you could turn a blank key into any key you needed, to use for all sorts of locks.

WordPress is kind of like that key machine. With it, you can unlock all kinds of websites: CMS (Content Management System), personal website, business website, online store, information site, you name it. It really is a key machine. But like that old key machine, it needs more – those extra parts (blank keys) to do the job.

In the WordPress world, those "extra parts" are plugins and widgets. These bits of code can change the generic WordPress site into a very targeted, and very powerful, website. So let's take a look at plugins and widgets, why they are so valuable, and most importantly, what ones are on the "must have" list for any well–run blog.

Wherefore Art Thou, Plugin (Or Widget)?

As I've already discussed, a plugin or widget is a bit of code that adds something extra to WordPress. In the last chapter I mentioned a plugin to hold automated comment programs (spammers) at bay, something WordPress has trouble doing when first set up.

That's only one example of what a plugin can do. Since they are programmed to interact with WordPress internally, they can do anything that WordPress itself can do, and more. So to understand plugins a bit better, let's look at how WordPress works, and how plugins "plug into" the program:

• When someone requests a blog page with their browser (for example, by visiting

---

your website with Google Chrome or Firefox), the request starts up the WordPress program code. This code is designed to figure out what page is supposed to be "served up", and then generates it (remember, in the WordPress world there is no real website, and everything is served up right away on demand, like a very fast short–order cook).

• Before WordPress decides which page to send back, it needs to set up a few things. Connecting to a database (since much of its data, including any articles, is stored there), and checking and cleaning up the requested URL (to prevent it being abused by hackers) are just two items. Another one is initializing all code, including those piggybacked code pieces, plugins and widgets (you might wonder how WordPress knows that these items are to be activated – in fact, the active or in–use items are stored in a list in the database).

To activate a plugin, all WordPress has to do at first is load it into its system. The plugin at that point takes care of the rest of its setup, and sends out software 'tendrils' to hook itself into WordPress. These tendrils, or hooks, are programming requests to be informed when something goes on; in effect, to keep the plugin "in the loop". For instance, in the comment filter plugin we've mentioned, one hook there is notified whenever a comment comes in, so that it can check whether it needs to be kept or deleted. So although they are called hooks, think of these more as the plugin sending out 'assistants' to a bunch of WordPress 'meetings'; these assistants report back when anything interesting happens in their meeting, and just sit around doing nothing otherwise.

There are many, many hooks in WordPress, and many ways the plugin can do its business. Once it's brought into WordPress by loading, it is as much a part of the code as anything else, free to do anything, good or bad, that it was designed for (more on the bad later).

And a widget? It's a later addition to the WordPress world, and is much like a plugin, set up and run the same way. However, widgets have a visual aspect to them: You can add them to themes and move them around on the blog. With a typical blog, much of the sidebar display you see is actually made up of widgets. WordPress includes some of these as built–in widgets, with optional external add-on widgets providing the rest.

> In fact, plugins and widgets are so closely related that when anyone speaks of plugins, they likely also mean widgets. After all, aside from a

bit of code to display itself on the theme, a widget is practically indistinguishable from a plugin. So from now on, I'll refer to 'plugin' to include both plugins and widgets, unless I specifically mean one or the other.

Plugin Or Widget Installation

Plugins and widgets can be created by anyone, and you get them (almost) anywhere. Key to using any of them are these steps:

• Getting a copy of it. This is in one of three ways: From the developer of the plugin/widget, from WordPress, or (sometimes) it's built-in the WordPress program and just needs to be activated (obviously, the easiest solution!)

If from an owner or developer: He/she may sell it, give it to you, or place it on their site for downloading. When you get it, you should get install instructions to follow as well.

From WordPress: WordPress has a collection of plugins from various authors stored on their website. From within the program you search, review and download them.

• Getting it to your blog. Plugins reside at a special location in a WordPress blog, a directory called /wp-content/plugins/ – place the code there, and WordPress can see it, presenting you with a pick list once you're in the Admin section (the PLUGINS menu). If you get the plugin directly from WordPress, it will copy the files there automatically.

• Starting it up. Called activating the plugin, this usually means a single click to set it up for WordPress use. From the PLUGINS menu in Admin, you have listed all the plugins WordPress 'sees'. To turn one on, you just click on the corresponding ACTIVATE link.

• Configuring it. For more complicated plugins, or for unusual setups, you may also have to go through a menu of options for that specific plugin, and tweak things to get it just right. Check the author's website for any setup information.

• For widgets, an extra step is to place it on your theme, and possibly adjust additional settings. For that, you go to the APPEARANCE; WIDGETS section. Widgets that are activated are displayed on the left hand side of the page. You click and drag them to columns on the right to place them; placing them there immediately activates them to display on the current theme. Often, you can also click on a button in the widget entry to open it, and add information or change settings.

As mentioned, one major repository for plugins and widgets is WordPress Central's Plugins directory itself, at

```
https://wordpress.org/plugins/
```

There, you can review many, many plugins, as well as install them easily, in a series of simple steps:

• From inside your own blog, you can go to the **PLUGINS; ADD NEW** submenu and use the **SEARCH** section to look for the plugin you want on WordPress.org.

• Your search results can be clicked on, either to get more information on it (the **MORE DETAILS** link), or to download it to your blog's plugin directory (**INSTALL NOW**). Click on the latter to download and install the plugin. That plugin is now present on your site, but not running; the remaining step is to activate it with the **ACTIVATE PLUGIN** link. From there, your plugin is active and ready to go – much easier than manually!

The FTP Option

Of course, not all plugins have that "special arrangement" with WordPress.org. Or, for one reason or another, you may want (or need) to install plugins directly. So for those situations, you'll manually install plugins using FTP.

With FTP, here's the steps you'll follow (we'll use the FileZilla program in this example):

• If this is the first time you've used FTP on your site, you'll need to configure FileZilla. Run the program, and in the **FILE** menu, go to **SITE MANAGER**. A dialog opens, and you can click on **NEW SITE** to create a new entry (feel free to name it).

• For the site, you'll need to enter a host (the domain name, but without the `http://` in front of it), and click on **NORMAL** where it says **LOGON TYPE**. This then lets you enter the password and user name to log into your site via FTP. All that information is usually given to you when you first sign up for an account with a web hosting company.

• Use the CONNECT button to save the information and log in. If there's no problems, you should be looking at the directory structure of your blog site (if there are problems, recheck your settings).

• You now have to download and unpack the plugin locally on your computer. Most of them are in the form of a single .zip file, which you'll need to 'un–zip' into individual files. If you don't have a tool for that, I recommend the free 7–Zip, from

```
http://www.7-zip.org/
```

• To upload a file, you'll need to set the source and destination. In the left panel of FileZilla is a Windows Explorer–style display, which you can use to find the local files to copy. In the right panel is a similar display, but for your website. Use that side to navigate around your site, until you've found the /wp-content/plugins/ directory for your blog.

• Find the unzipped plugin files on your computer by using the left panel of FileZilla, and then click and drag the files from the left to the right to copy them onto your website.

• When copying is done (the Task List, located in FileZilla's bottom panel, empties), you can close FileZilla down.

As you can see, the newer method of installing plugins is much easier! Nonetheless, FTP is a vital technique to understand, and useful for many other tasks besides plugin installation. Give it a try, and if you have any problems, there are plenty of tutorials on the topic online.

Gun (And Plugin) Safety – Ready…, Fire!, Aim?

I've explained the basics of using plugins and widgets on your site, given you a way to grab any– and every– one you might be interested in, and made your blog easier to add functionality to.

So, perhaps it's a little late to warn you NOT to use plugins!

Frankly, every discussion about plugins should begin with "unless you really, really need this, don't install this plugin…" There are some good reasons to avoid "plugin madness", adding lots of plugins to your WordPress blog:

• Each plugin piggybacks into WordPress, adding to the workload of the server program and CPU (computer). One or two is fine; fifty can be a performance penalty to your web server's computer, and really slow it down.

• Plugins can be poorly written. There's usually a fast way and a slow way to do anything in WordPress. Avoid the plugins that choose the slow way. Not only have I seen code that is downright sluggish and poorly designed, but I've seen code that is unsafe. So skip the hassles by avoiding as many plugins as you can.

• Plugins go out of date. Sadly, few people can make a living writing WordPress plugins, since everyone expects free software. For this and other reasons, plugins are not always updated. And since code typically has bugs in it (including security problems that hackers may make use of), it's important that they be updated regularly. If that's not the case for a particular plugin, then it's a plugin you're best not using, unless you are comfortable fixing it yourself.

• Every time WordPress changes to a new version, plugins break. Well written plugins should have no problems (usually), but the more you have, the more chances one or two will hiccup, and you'll need to deal with it immediately.

• Plugins can be malicious.

The last point is the biggy: Plugins can be downright bad for your site's health. Every plugin you install is like inviting a person into your house and handing them the keys. That person then has 24/7 access to your house – while you're sleeping, busy elsewhere, vacationing, etc.

For most plugins, this is not an issue. But this power means a malicious programmer can write a plugin that does all kinds of things to your site. For instance:

• A plugin has access to your WordPress install, which means it can add a new user and delete your old one, effectively locking you out of your own blog!

• Likewise, it has access to all your data in the database.

• Plugins can 'see' around the physical website as easily as the blog itself. If you give a malicious plugin developer permission, anything on your site is visible and accessible, including password files, data files, and more.

• PHP, the programming language of plugins and WordPress, has a great deal of power. A plugin could easily email everyone and anyone if it wanted, and become a spam relay – if you install the wrong plugin.

Now, I'm not saying every plugin is out to get you. In all the time I've worked with WordPress, I haven't come across a single deliberately malicious plugin. However, I've come across poorly written ones, which just shifts the blame: Instead of a nasty programmer, you have a programmer's mistakes being used by nasty hackers.

> What I mention here about plugins also applies to widgets, of course; however, it especially applies to themes, since they are likewise made of programming code, and have just as much access to your site as any plugin. Moreover, themes actually ARE being hacked regularly to do nasty things, a subject I'll discuss in more detail in the chapter on themes.

A badly written plugin can be like that friend you gave your keys to; he's honest, but he keeps forgetting to lock the door at night. And unlike the real world, where bad guys have limited time to cruise up and down streets to see if doors are unlocked, on the Internet, they can run programs that check sites out night and day, looking for any weakness.

Because of that, I'd rather you have a healthy respect for what can be done, than assume there's no problems. So here's some tips for safe plugin use:

• As I mentioned, use the minimum number of plugins to do the job. It will cut down your stress level in many, many, ways.

• Like anything on the Internet, avoid bad neighborhoods. If you're nervous about the website, then why download and run plugin code from it?

• Try to find plugins that are maintained regularly. If the author has given up support, try to find a similar (active) plugin and use it instead. New security problems (called security exploits) happen often, so you don't want old software on your site if you can help it.

• Likewise, if you have unused plugins on your site, remove them, either via a direct delete with FTP (deactivating them first from inside WordPress, of course) or using the plugin's DELETE link beside each plugin entry (shown via the PLUGINS menu). Inactive plugins may not be connected to WordPress, but they are still part of your website, and they still have code in them. And that code can be called directly via a URL. While it's unlikely they will ever cause any problems, why not avoid the risk, and remove them from your site.

• Use WordPress.org for plugins – but don't depend on it. The plugin listings on WordPress.org are vast, with tens of thousands of entries, and no one can manually review all of them. My recommendation is to stick to plugins that are by popular and well–known authors, that have a large number of downloads, and that people seem happy with (that is, rated high on the site). A brand new plugin from an unknown programmer, even if it provides great features, may not be worth the hassle.

Plugins and widgets provide tremendous possibilities for your blog, but a healthy respect for them will make your site maintenance much easier.

And in fact, I practice what I preach: The rest of this chapter deals with a very short list of "must have" plugins I use, the minimum ones you'll need to add to your blog. So let's look at the plugins and widgets that just about any site will end up needing.

Plugin: Spam Control

We've already touched on the issue of comment spam control. This plugin, called "Cookies for Comments", works by setting up code normally not read by spam robots; this fact is used to filter out their messages quite effectively.

To get it, search on the name "Cookies for Comments" in the search box of the PLUGINS; ADD NEW submenu. When you find it, click on INSTALL NOW beside its entry, then ACTIVATE PLUGIN to get it running.

From there, you can do a bit of plugin–specific editing; you'll go to the SETTINGS; COOKIES FOR COMMENTS submenu (the plugin adds this new menu entry to WordPress when activated). There is only one question there, "What should happen to comments caught by CFC?". By default, they will go to the spam folder. If you wish, you can have them automatically deleted by selecting that option from the drop–down box, and then clicking on SAVE OPTIONS to set it.

From then on, any computer–generated spam comments will never appear on your blog, but will be handled transparently by this plugin – a real boon for busy blogs (and webmasters)!

Plugin: Contact Form (And Other Forms)

For many web pages on your site, like legal information or your About page, you only need to create a page in WordPress, and put in the necessary text. Unfortunately, a contact form is interactive, and so you need a plugin to handle it. They can be as simple as a form asking for an email address (to reply to) and a comment box, to full–bodied forms with multiple fields for business use.

If you do a plugin search on "contact form", you'll find many to choose from. They usually offer a simple interface, and require a page (not post) to be set up, including a special keyword in the post to activate the contact form. Here's an example of using one, "WPForms":

• As with the comment plugin, search for it, install it, and then activate it.

• You will be taken to a page where you can create a form ("Create Your First Form" button). From that page "Select a Template" choose "Simple Contact Form". For now, just save that form, and then click on "Embed".

• The Embed button will display a code like this – copy it:

```
[wpforms id="9999" title="false" description="false"]
```

• Create a page entry via PAGE; ADD NEW. Make the title something obvious, like "Contact" or "Contact Us", and paste the code you just copied into the body of the page. Publish the page.

• Once published, you can view the finished page on your blog, ready to accept submissions. Do a test of it by sending yourself a message, confirming it arrived in your email inbox.

Feel free to try other contact form plugins, since the procedure is very similar; however, for simplicity, this one will get you up and running (and receiving messages) quickly!

Plugin: Search Engine Optimization

Search Engine Optimization (SEO) is a vital area for your blog to shine in. It means making every aspect of your blog enticing for search engines, and easy for them to categorize in their search engine listings.

One popular plugin to manage this is "Yoast SEO". We'll look at using it in detail in a later chapter, but for convenience we'll explain here how to set it up for basic use – just follow these steps:

• Search on "Yoast" via the P**LUGINS**; A**DD** N**EW** submenu, install, and activate.

• When active, it will prompt you to use the wizard. You can do so, and if you're comfortable with that, then set up everything from there. One option is just to accept the defaults, and then go through the menu options in detail later, tweaking as needed.

Once set up, it's ready to use. We'll explore it in more detail in the chapter on SEO.

Plugin: Site Mapping

At one time, search engines welcomed a sitemap alongside your blog, a special file that listed all the pages, making it easy to index. However, as time went by, it became less important, partly because search engines have gotten quite good at finding pages without help, and partly because WordPress organizes posts so well, making them very easy to find.

So, while in the past I would have recommended a Sitemap plugin to get your site indexed faster, I won't in this edition. Frankly, I haven't used Sitemapping plugins in a long, long time, and without them, I still can get sites indexed within days.

However, if you are determined to have a site map generated, go to the P**LUGINS** menu option and click on the A**DD** N**EW** button, then search on 'sitemap'. Pick one of the results, install it following the directions for that particular plugin. That's it!

Plugin: Database Backup

If your blog went down tomorrow, how much effort would it take you to get it up and running again, with all the text reentered? If it's more than a few minutes, then you need a backup. Your database contains just about every component that makes your blog unique (except for plugins and themes), and so it's a must to perform regular backups of it.

"WP DB Backup" takes care of the details, emailing you a backup on a schedule so you always have a recent copy. To use it, follow these steps:

• Search on "**WP DB Backup**", install, and activate.

• Go to the settings menu at T**OOLS**; B**ACKUP**, and check the details. By default, it will save the core database files, but you may wish to check other entries on the right side, to save additional files (for example, a database table created by a plugin).

• To test it out, under **BACKUP OPTIONS**, click the button **BACKUP NOW** to process the files and give you a database copy in a few moments. The file will be packaged (compressed) in `.tqz` format, similar to `.zip` – you can unpack it using programs like Winzip or 7-Zip.

• Once downloading works, you can schedule your backup. Check the tables you want in the lower section labeled **SCHEDULED BACKUP**, and confirm the email address is correct. Also check a timing entry: I recommend at least **ONCE WEEKLY**, but **ONCE DAILY** may be preferable if you write a lot. Then click on **SCHEDULE BACKUP** to set it up. At regular intervals, you'll receive the compressed package of database files via email, ready to reuse in an emergency. Note that the contents, called an SQL file, may require that you ask a WordPress 'Guru' for help if you do need to use it in an emergency – but that's still easier (and cheaper) than recreating the website from scratch!

Plugin: Caching And Optimization

This plugin is not always needed, especially on smaller blogs – but when it is needed, it is extremely welcome.

One of Donncha O Caoimh's WordPress plugins (he also wrote the "Cookies for Comments" spam plugin), "WP Super Cache" is a plugin that stores a complete image of each WordPress page for a limited time. Remember I said that WordPress works by generating a page on the fly like a short–order cook? Well, that cook has only so many hands – too many orders, and he can break down. Likewise, a popular website can break down with too many web page requests. By storing a completed image of various pages, this plugin offloads some of the processing work that WordPress does (think of it as that cook defrosting a meal now and then instead of creating everything from scratch).

To use it:

• Search on "WP Super Cache", install, and activate.

• In the new submenu **SETTINGS; WP SUPER CACHE** you'll see the plugin settings. Check "Caching On" at the top and click on **UPDATE STATUS** to set it up.

• Now pages will be saved (cached) the first time they are viewed by someone, and passed to you via that cache from then on. This continues for about an hour after that first page view, then the cache empties, and the cycle starts all over again with the next page view.

Refresh your home page a couple of times. The result is that first page view will be the usual speed, but the subsequent ones will be fast – exactly why WP Super Cache helps with busy sites!

> The Super Cache plugin, because it stores a copy of each page, can make it a problem to troubleshoot your site, since changes may take awhile to show up! For this reason, if you do use it, remember to turn it off before working on your site for whatever reason. Also, make sure to use the CACHING OFF setting in the SETTINGS; **WP SUPER CACHE** submenu rather than deactivating it via the **PLUGINS** menu. Note the plugin won't interfere with normal operations like posting articles; only maintenance, such as setting up a plugin or widget, or changing a theme.

Summary

This chapter doesn't cover every plugin you conceivably might need – just a good selection of the ones you'll frequently need. Specialty sites may require other plugins. If that's your case, do a search online, verify the plugin is good to use, and give it a try. After all, the power of WordPress plugins means YOU control what your blog does – and how it does it!

Attract Visitors With Your Theme

We all see with little detectors in our eyes, called cones and rods. The rods, numbering over 100 million, help detect light; the cones however, numbering about 6–7 million, are what give us color viewing. In effect, our eyes are 7 megapixel cameras – each!

Not only that, but the eye moves constantly, and the brain can integrate those moving images so that we don't see just 7 megapixel images – we see much more. For instance, can you make out a telephone line on a pole in the distance? It's actually too small to register on a single cone, yet the brain can take a moving image across several cones and integrate it into a picture of the line.

With such high–powered optical equipment included in each and every one of us as standard features, it's no wonder we are visually oriented. And that visual orientation comes in handy when we discuss WordPress, because it provides a way for everyone to express their individuality on their blogs – with colorful themes.

What Exactly Are Themes?

Themes are everything to WordPress – in fact, when you look at a blog, all you are seeing is the theme. A theme can make a blog look like just about anything. For instance, themes can make the blog look like a news site, a personal blog (obviously), a sales page for a product, a store, and much more.

Like a plugin, a theme is PHP code that WordPress includes inside itself when running. Unlike a plugin however, it is display oriented. In fact, if you look at a theme, you'll see that while it has PHP code in it, there's mostly web display code like HTML (or XHTML, HTML's stricter, younger, sibling), and CSS (Cascading Style Sheets, code used to style a page easily).

In a way, a theme is like a mini program to WordPress. Actually, it's a cluster of mini programs, because WordPress isn't limited to a single file for page display; all the files in the theme directory can contribute. That's the reason your blog's home page can look different from an individual post page – it actually is, using a different theme 'program' for its display.

By default, WordPress when installed uses a specific theme, which changes from time to time, and the theme files are all in a single directory on the blog website, in the `/wp-content/themes/twentyten/` directory (all themes must be in a subdirectory off of the `/wp-content/themes/` directory to be seen and used by WordPress).

This default theme consists (usually) of the following groups of files:

• The main blog design page, called `index.php` – this is the code that displays the home page of your blog.

• Design pages for posts (`single.php`), pages (`page.php`), category and author displays (`category.php`, `author.php`), among others.

• Support page information, parts that are reused across pages but are not full web pages themselves, like `sidebar.php`, used to group all sidebar code for every page into one place, `footer.php`, and `header.php`, which handle the footer and header code, respectively. Besides the size savings of keeping these sections in single files for all web pages to reuse, it also means that changes are easier to make, since an edit to the single `footer.php` file is immediately reflected in all the web pages using that file.

• A style sheet for the theme style, called `style.css`

• A series of header images stored in the `/images/headers/` subdirectory.

• Extra support files the theme designer might want to use. For example, the `functions.php` file is used to provide more functionality or options to the specific theme.

Used together, these PHP files are called one by one for each web page, and their job is to format that page properly, usually by setting up the sidebar, a main section, a header, footer, etc., as well as formatting one or more articles so they look nice on that resulting page.

For example, say you are looking at a single post, perhaps by clicking on an article link from the home page. To produce that web page, WordPress will do something like this:

• Find out which theme it is using, and make sure it looks into the correct subdirectory of /wp-content/themes/ for the files it needs.

• Look for a file to display the single post (single.php), and run it like a program (note that some themes lack this file; if so, it will run index.php instead).

• When single.php runs, the theme designer has programmed code to display the page, but also to format the text, display the header, footer, and so forth (it does these by running header.php and footer.php). For instance, one bit of code is to display specific article information, like the article title, the publication date, and of course, the article itself, each of which is generated by asking WordPress for data.

So you see, every theme is a bundle of PHP files, artwork, and a style sheet, placed online for WordPress to 'run' as needed. The theme package will all fit into a directory, and this directory is uploaded to the /wp-content/themes/ directory and placed there, via FTP or direct download from WordPress (yes, they do automatic theme installs as well as plugins).

Once in place, you can log into Admin, go to the **APPEARANCE; THEMES** submenu and view the themes. Most themes include a small thumbnail image to show what they look like; some older themes may be missing that. Pick the one that you want, click on the **PREVIEW** link below it to see a sample display, or click on the **ACTIVATE** link to activate it, making it the newest 'look' for your blog. Just a note about security: **PREVIEW** actually loads and runs the theme, so avoid even previewing a hacked or potentially hacked theme.

The subject of themes is a deep one, and there's plenty to explore. For now, just remember that someone should give you a complete package that fits into a directory like /default/ or /twentyten/, and should have all the files for your design, ready to activate.

Default Or Different? Paid Or Free? Old Or New?

Every WordPress blog is installed with the default theme, which is quite nice. You don't need to change it at all if you want, but most people want to – and WordPress designers around the world have provided a wide variety to choose from!

The default theme is perfect if you are a 'traditional' blog user, such as a blog writer, and your goal is to write a blog about life, or something similar. But an online store looks different from a personal blog, and a company site looks different from an online store (unless it is a store, of course). So you'll want another theme for them.

In choosing a theme, one thing is easy: Paid or free. Over the years, I've preferred recommending free themes. However, there is a nasty trend out there for 'someone' to add hacked code to the theme (Theme designers? Sites that offer free themes? Like most crimes, it's hard to know who exactly is doing the crime, only that it IS happening). This code, like code in plugins, exposes your site to a wide variety of nasty surprises. Yet unlike plugins, where the issue is theoretical, themes are routinely hacked.

What is a hacked theme like? In a recent example, I grabbed a well–known theme to modify for a family site. In the `footer.php` file was code resembling this:

```
<?php eval(gzinflate(base64_decode("3YbaXxc2VCEh2zaLzTY7S83LNNnkgJRMbf
    =B3HttGpraEvxoKun57nfl5XMmwXMmwXMmwRD5izterH31T2M32UN37DteULCuCLpDwa
    dcP2GMRFGAWAvmUtdTw7RtMgSMhAa0A"))); ?>
```

This is a typical way to hide PHP code from view. While in itself it's not bad (I've used it myself to obscure some of my custom code), in this case what it hid was code that would "call out" to a home site, and then download files to your website without you knowing, files that would let it take over your blog if it wished (or insert ads for Viagra and the like).

To make matters worse, this hidden code also included some vital HTML for the site, so simply removing it would break the theme. It needed careful surgery to remove it, while still letting the theme 'live'.

In fact, many times when people claim their sites have been hacked, a theme is the culprit. Unfortunately, when a theme hack occurs, there's no easy solution except to completely scrub the site, delete everything, and start over. Otherwise, code like the example I mentioned could easily place itself in some far–off location on your website, ready to go active again once you've cleaned up.

Because of the commonness of this problem, and the seriousness of it, I now steer away from recommending free themes, unless you can have someone competent check the theme over and verify it (much like I did for the theme I had – once cleaned up, it was fine to use). For that reason, I now recommend paying someone else, either to clean up a theme you have an eye on, or to order a paid–for theme outright.

I cannot repeat myself enough here – NEVER use a free theme without getting it checked out! Either you pay someone to look over your theme, you pay for a custom (non–free) theme, or you pay to get your site cleaned up after you've been hacked – sadly, nowadays these seem to be the only choices.

Finding The Theme Of Your Dreams

So where do you get themes? A quick search online for "WordPress themes" (or "free WordPress themes") will give you lists upon lists.

If you have a WordPress guru handy, then checking these over or modifying a theme should be no problem. In any case, there is a good chance you'll want to tweak your theme, requiring a professional's help; so you'll be hiring someone more than likely anyways.

If however you have no one currently, here's a trick: Find a paid–for theme you like the look of, and ask the author their charge to make the changes you want, as well as the theme order price. You get a designer who knows the theme inside out, and you get a paid theme that avoids the hacking issues I've mentioned. Plus, there's a very good chance the designer will do minor modifications at little or no cost, saving you even more. But even if it does cost you, his or her work will still be faster than anyone else, since they know the theme!

For the free route, there is one more caution – old themes versus new themes. In the old days of WordPress, themes were not as complicated, and many of them had a single design for the main blog page, which was reused (with minor changes) throughout the website. For those, there were no individual `pages.php`, `single.php` and so on, just one large `index.php` (as I pointed out earlier, if these individual pages aren't present, WordPress "falls back" to `index.php`). As well, those theme designs existed before widgets became available, so they would not be widget enabled.

But some of the old designs are very nice, and hard to pass up. In that case, besides the obligatory hacker file scanning, you'll need to ask your theme guru to 'widgetize' the theme, and optionally create the separate pages for each web page view (while not strictly necessary, doing this can make modifications easier later).

Additionally, they could split out the `index.php` file into the sidebar, header and footer files. These files then become the only copy of each section, no matter how many theme pages you add. This can make modifications easier as well, since (for example) one change to the header file will affect the header on all pages.

What's In A Good Theme?

What makes a good theme? Pretty, easy to read, flexible?

Unfortunately, while these are important features, on the Internet there's a bigger one – search engine optimized. And an "SEO theme" is vital to your website.

Why is SEO so important? Partly because search engines rule the world online. Many sites get huge chunks of traffic from search engine queries, and THAT traffic tends to type something into a search engine, click on items on the first page of results, and leave it at that (or go on to a new search). So for that reason, getting on the first page, and especially near the top of that page, means a great deal of extra traffic for you.

To work best with SEO, a theme should have some minimal features:

• Internal HTML should be designed for SEO. Many themes make the blog's title at the top an <h1> tag, indicating it is the most important text on the page. Rarely is this the actual case with the web page; more likely the most important text is the title of the article, and so it should be <h1>, instead of <h2> or <h3>, which is usually the case with blog themes. The good news is it's possible to fix this by simply removing the <h1> entry, leaving the <h2> for the article title as the highest rank on the page (by default it then becomes the most important text).

Over the years, I've recommended two ways to accomplish this: Editing the HTML and CSS to display the blog title the same way it currently does, but without the <h1> tag; and replacing the text with graphical text, which is still readable by people but is ignored by search engines. Which you choose depends on whether you consider your blog title "keyword rich" or not. If it is, leave the text in; but if not, turn it into a graphic and let the search engines focus elsewhere on the page.

• It should be light. Too many web designers make a design pretty first, then efficient afterward (if at all). The result is a theme that's a big drain on a web server, and so makes it hard to run the website. Watch out for extra database accesses in the theme, lengthy style sheets, complicated display code, lots of JavaScript, or large images. One way to test it is to check out the theme on a sample site, and repeatedly load pages. If they feel sluggish or parts load oddly, don't expect anything to be better when it appears on your site.

While much of this can be solved by using a caching plugin like the one discussed in the last chapter, not all sins are curable that way. Caching works on repeated loads of the same page, and does poorly if a lot of different pages are loaded. So be aware that you may pay for that extremely pretty theme by needing to move to a larger, more powerful (and more expensive) web server!

• It should have the most important content near the front. Search engines place more emphasis on the earlier part of a web page. In fact, on large pages they can stop scanning before the end, leaving off the remainder of the page's content. For many themes, this is easily accomplished by placing the article column physically before the sidebar in the HTML code for the theme. With the careful use of CSS display code, the physical position of the HTML needn't matter for viewers, since you can use CSS to rearrange how everything fits together (placing that column on the left or right side, for instance), and so please both your eyes and the search engines.

• It should be easily customizable. If the theme has an image, it should be simple to replace it with something else. The previous WordPress Default theme was a bad example of this, since the header image was also part of the blog frame, and hard to adjust; the new theme is much better, using an image–only header you can replace with similarly–sized artwork.

Also, if there is a menu, it should not be "hard–coded" with values that don't matter (for instance, a link to their site instead of yours). And any text on the page should ideally be adjustable, and not fixed. Although you can edit the theme directly, it's much nicer if you don't have to, and can instead make changes via WordPress Admin.

• It should be standards compliant. One standard you'll hear a lot about is from the W3C (World Wide Web Consortium), which involves the syntax of web page code that is correct and error–free (think of it as proper grammar for web pages). Search engines can and do index pages that aren't standards compliant; however, a compliant theme indicates someone knows what they are doing, and reduces the chance of pages indexed poorly because they were broken. But note that a theme is only part of the equation: As you add widgets and articles, there's always the chance that they may introduce some 'breaks' in the web page that are not the fault of the theme. Obviously, the theme designer can't fix your widgets and articles, so it's important to check a theme over before loading it up with your goodies. The easiest way to test any theme is to activate it on a site, and enter the home page URL into the W3C validation form at

```
http://validator.w3.org/
```

Its response will tell you how 'compliant' your theme is.

• It should have a reasonable license. While I have no problem with paid themes, the license must match your needs. If you plan to reuse the theme many times, the license must permit this, as opposed to a single–site or single–use license. It definitely pays to check before you buy, since some themes can limit you to a specific domain, and even prevent reselling, so if you sell your site to someone else, the new owner may legally need to purchase the theme again.

Obviously, the more of these items that are already dealt with when you get your theme, the better. And even though I stress search engine optimization, it's important to remember that's only part of the equation: Ultimately, it's real, live, money–paying people who will make or break your site, and a theme has to keep their needs in mind, too.

The Pizzazz Factor

So getting traffic to your site is one thing: What about when they arrive? Here's where "people factors" come into play, such as:

• A nice design, with easy to read text. I once saw a site with light gray text on a white background – why do that? If it's hard to read, visitors will use their browser's Back button and continue the search. Your theme's goal is to make it easier to click on the scroll bar and read more of the article than it is to click on the Back button!

• Familiarity and appearance. People shy away from ugly sites, so you need an inviting theme. As well, we work with what's familiar. So, a business site should look like a business site, and a store should look like a store.

• Specific features for specific uses. If you plan to use Google AdSense on your site to make money, then you'll likely want a theme that can easily include multiple ads, or at least is easy to edit to add the code yourself. Widgetized themes, as already mentioned, mean you get the flexibility of placing items in the sidebar, like email forms, rather than manually editing the theme itself.

• Many themes today use pictures for each article, which can really enhance a site visually. Displaying the picture is one thing; understanding HOW to display the picture is another. If the theme uses pictures for each post, it should have clear information on how to add your photos, and how to set up anything needed to run this theme feature. Alternately, if you don't want to use the pictures (or don't want to spend all that time adding them), can the feature be disabled?

• Is there enough (but not too much) widget 'room'? Many themes are widget enabled not just for a single sidebar, but anywhere a flexible display is required. While a lot of widget space is great, there can be a problem if you don't have enough to fill them! In that case, turning off a section or minimizing it so it doesn't distract would be a key feature to have.

As a final point, you'll want your theme to be editable, because no matter how often a theme advertises itself as "one size fits all", there will be times you'll want to tweak a thing or two. And for that, you'll need to dig into the theme code itself – the topic of our next section.

Editing Your Themes

Themes are code; and code can be edited on your computer and uploaded. Sounds simple, right?

It can be. In WordPress Admin, you just click on **APPEARANCE; EDITOR** to view your theme in an editor.

Now when you're in a hurry, it's easy to look at that and think you can bypass the download/backup/edit/upload sequence I mentioned earlier for editing WordPress files. And it IS faster.

But the first time you make a mistake in this window, and break your theme, and your site goes dead while you frantically try to find a good copy of the theme and upload it, you'll wish you had listened to me. I know – there's been far too many times I wish I'd listened to me, too. Nothing quite matches the sinking feeling of possibly, maybe, likely, destroying your site. So avoid it with careful editing on your local computer.

Another reason for editing locally is that some text editors use syntax highlighting, a very nice way of moving throughout the text and understanding the parts. For instance, a theme can have four computer languages mixed up on a page: CSS parts, HTML parts, PHP parts, and possibly even JavaScript. A good syntax editor (like

Notepad++, mentioned earlier), will show keywords in a different color, and will help you pick out the parts of the page so that you can edit easily.

This syntax highlighting is a great boon when you want to dig into your theme. Many themes intermingle primarily PHP and HTML/CSS, and keeping track of which is which at any point can be problematic.

For example, here's a snippet of code from a typical theme, with the PHP sections underlined (the rest is HTML code):

```
<body <?php body_class(); ?>>
<div id="wrapper" class="hfeed">
 <div id="header">
  <div id="masthead">
   <div id="branding">
    <?php if ( is_home() || is_front_page() ) { ?>
     <h1 id="site-title"><span><a href="<?php echo home_url( '/' ); ?>"
    title="<?php echo esc_attr( get_bloginfo( 'name', 'display' ) ); ?>"
    rel="home"><?php bloginfo( 'name' ); ?></a></span></h1>
    <?php } else { ?>
     <div id="site-title"><span><a href="<?php echo home_url( '/' ); ?>"
    title="<?php echo esc_attr( get_bloginfo( 'name', 'display' ) ); ?>"
    rel="home"><?php bloginfo( 'name' ); ?></a></span></div>
    <?php } ?>
    <div id="site-description"><?php bloginfo( 'description' ); ?></div>
```

As you can see from this mishmash of PHP and HTML, color coding would really help!

Why care? Because when you edit, you must stay within the boundaries of HTML and PHP. Mixing them up is about the easiest way to break a theme.

One aid to make it easier is to check for start and end tags in PHP. In most themes, look for <?php and ?>, although some themes might use <? and ?> instead; notice the underlined sections in the code example all started with <?php and ended with ?>. Inside those tags is PHP; outside, HTML. And if you get it wrong, your theme has problems (of course, to further confuse matters, it IS legal to leave off the closing ?> at the very end of the file; in that case, everything from the last <?php until the file's end is considered PHP code, blank lines and all).

Take for example this bit of PHP, which echos (displays) the word in quotes, 'hi':

```
echo "hi";
```

If you entered this into the HTML side of the theme, it would likely display the whole text on the web page (including the quotes and semicolon, and the word 'echo'). The solution then is to surround it with the proper tags, like this:

```
<?php echo "hi"; ?>
```

On the other hand, inserting HTML into the PHP side of things would be a different problem, such as adding this line break code:

```
<br>
```

Putting it inside the PHP code would break the theme, and give you an error message like:

```
syntax error, unexpected '<' in file 'something_or_other.php' at line 99
```

In this case, you can usually 'escape' the surrounding PHP by using the tags in reverse:

```
?> <br> <?php
```

As you can see, even with a little edit like this, theme tweaking can get complicated. All the more reason to spend time getting the best possible theme before you use it – because the time the theme designer spends is time you won't have to!

Themes are a vital part of your website, and a good theme pays for itself in helping you put your "best foot forward" online. With a bit of attention and care (and this chapter's tricks), you're well on your way to getting a theme that will maximize your site's impact, both for people and search engines.

Pay Attention To SEO – Or Risk Your Site Being Ignored!

"If you build a better mousetrap, the world will beat a path to your door."

Don't believe it.

I once saw a better mousetrap. It was a square tube that slanted up at the back, and had a latched door on the front. The mouse crawled in, and moved to the back to get the food. This tilted the tube backwards, and the front door latched shut. Humane and effective, it was much better than the Spring of Death style everyone uses.

And where did I see it? In the bargain bin at a dollar store!

The same thing happens online. You may have the best site of its kind out there; so why doesn't the world beat a path to your door?

The fact is, the best things aren't automatically out there for all to see, and you need promotion, no matter how good the idea is.

Fortunately, WordPress does take care of one aspect of site promotion: With its built–in article management and advertising (via RSS feeds and pinging) the world is told about what you have. But getting search engines to visit is only part of the issue.

In the last chapter we discussed why SEO is so important. Simply put, search engines will place you in their listings; but by using search engine optimization, you might move your listings from the far back to the first page – maybe even the first entry on the first page.

What is the magic behind this? Just coming up with what search engines want, and that ends up being what people want from search engines. So to understand how to get better rankings, let's first look at how people interact with search engines.

The Key To Search Engines – YOU

When you are looking for something, how do you search for it? If you're like most people, studies show you start broadly searching, and then narrow your focus.

This is natural, since when we are just wondering about something, general questions are good at finding out general information. But when we are start to focus, it's because we now know exactly what to search for.

For example, I was wondering about water purification some time ago. I knew a bit about it, but what I wanted was a solution for my home that wasn't invasive (no plumber needed, no pipes cut, easy to install myself, etc.) But first I had to understand what options were out there. So I typed phrases like this:

```
water purification
water purification cheap
water purification simple
water purification safe
```

From there, I found out that 'filter' was a more common term than 'purification'; also, a tap filter was the most likely option, as the other solutions, such as reverse osmosis, usually required pipes cut. So my next searches were more focused. Plus, now I would ask about pricing, since I was getting ready to buy:

```
water filter types
water filter pricing
water filter easy to install
```

This type of search has been duplicated billions of times by millions of people, in that we start from general questions and then narrow down as we get answers. While not true for absolutely everyone, it does seem to fit the case most times, and if we want to market successfully we need to realize that. Because as this simple example showed, general information is the start, but very focused answers to questions are the 'payday' end result.

And by placing these 'key' words on our web pages, we get indexed for them, and from there, search engine traffic comes our way. In this case, if I had a web page for "water filter types", search engines would list me for those searches, and visitors to my page would get information on filters. Plus, if I was smart, there would be an ad or two for filters on the page, with commissions for me!

What Goes Into A Keyword Or Phrase?

Of course, getting ranked well (placed high in the search engine listings) for a phrase involves a lot more details than simply putting words on a web page. These include:

• How popular a phrase is. If 100 million sites all deal with water filtration, then I have a lot of competition. If only 25,000 then it gets better. The good news is that throughout the blog you create, many pages will exist, and these pages will have many different phrases used, so you'll have more 'shots' at your search engine listings target.

• How generic a phrase is. As my example showed, we can add words to make a search more specific; after all, "water" can mean many things, while "water filtration" is fewer. So it makes sense that there are fewer sites for the longer, more specific term, and that means less competition. Fortunately, we'll still index for "water", so nothing is missed out (although since that is a popular word, don't expect high rankings for it!)

• How focused a phrase is. This goes hand in hand with longer or less generic phrases. If there is no ambiguity with a phrase, and everyone who types it in expects the same thing, then that is a great phrase to use. In this case, "water filtration" is still somewhat ambiguous: Is it filtration products for the home, the topic of municipal filtration, outdoor techniques (filtering clean water when camping) or something else? So even here, the phrase can be more specific and targeted.

• How your site treats a phrase. This is another topic too few discuss: Google takes the whole site into account when judging a keyword or phrase. If your blog is full of content on water filtration, talking about sports won't make you popular in that category; it doesn't work that way. But if you talk about other aspects of water treatment, then you improve your chances of ranking high with a new phrase. Generally speaking, the more focused a site's topic, the better Google ranks it as an authority site, that is, one it suggests to searchers, which also means higher rankings in search engine listings.

And if those items aren't enough, there's one more: Picking phrases that are linked to sales.

What Searchers REALLY Want

Psychology affects search engine rankings. Not all phrases mean the same thing to

---

people, and also what people look for in general is not the same as what they look for when getting ready to buy (for instance, water purification devices). So if you target the wrong phrase, you risk offering information to people not interested in purchasing, instead of going for phrases potential buyers use.

For instance, I could likely get a search entry to my page if I write an article about "water filtration", using those words. I might even have my article listed in Google high enough that it's on the first page when someone searches for "water filtration". But more than likely, the person reading it will then continue on in their search, because of the general nature of the question.

How about the alternative? I write an article on "water filter pricing"; now, when people are more ready to buy, these phrases (and their search engine listings) might lead to a purchase on my site.

In fact, what if I write both of these articles, and get both sets of readers? And as they search, they come back to my site often enough that eventually they skip Google, and just search directly? Then when they want to buy, they've been browsing through my site for some time, I've possibly built a relationship, and they are more inclined to follow my ads.

This is the key to SEO. It's not enough to have words that match searches on your page – it's necessary that they be the RIGHT words!

So you should balance your site's articles with both general and specific information. No one wants to visit a site that is all sell, sell, sell. As well, articles that don't seem to be a sales pitch tend to come across as more authoritative (something to do with the way we humans are wired), therefore adding content that is strictly informative is a good way to get more traffic, and keep everyone happy.

A final aspect of search engine optimization is the actual search engine entry, what the searcher sees in Google. That little blurb there can make or break your search engine efforts, since if it doesn't entice the viewer to your site then it might as well not be there.

It may seem tricky to get all this right, but we just need to handle a few items:

• Finding our site's focus.

• Picking good keywords for our articles and target audiences.

• Making sure we put our "best foot forward" in our search engine entries.

We'll start with targeting our website, and finding our site's niche.

What IS A Niche?

Niches are small groups. On the Internet, a niche is an area of understanding that is narrowly focused.

For instance, "dogs" isn't really a niche on the Internet, as it's too broad a subject. "Dog toys" is getting narrower, and closer to a niche. "Dog teething toys" does the job though; and "young dog teething toys" has it really pinpointed into a small group – yet still big enough for the Internet, with its millions of Information Superhighway 'Travelers'. In fact, that phrase returned about half a million results in Google!

The advantage of narrowing down into a niche like this is cost. For example, look at a company selling pet supplies; they can afford to advertise any and every dog product (and cat products as well). Big stores, with big budgets, make it very difficult to compete with them across a large group of items.

But in niches, the "little guy" still has a chance. You can focus on a narrow topic like "dog teething toys", and talk about it in detail. In contrast, the big company that tries to be that in–depth on everything related to dogs would quickly spend huge amounts of time and money trying to be "everything to everyone".

Of course, there's more to niche markets than that. It involves finding the keywords people are searching on, while making sure there isn't too much competition for their attention (other websites on "dog teething toys", for example).

It also involves making your site search engine friendly, so you can get more of that free traffic (as opposed to spending for advertising). This requires not only finding a niche to target, but creating content there that makes the search engines see you as an 'authority' on the topic – and which in turn gets you higher rankings.

You'll notice that with these examples I focus on money–making items. This highlights a mistake many people make: You are on the Internet to make money, so you need to always ask yourself when researching, what do buyers search for? While you can spend all your energy and time coming up with generic phrases that people search on (and then do little else), what you really want is a visitor to visit your page, read the article, nod their head, and then click on your ad next to the article, or buy your report, or sign up to your list.

One way of doing this is with practical goal–oriented articles and content. Don't just write about the many dog toys out there; write about the best ones, and use brand names. Mention what to look for in toys, and offer recommendations (honest ones, of course). And if that seems a bit awkward or crass to you, remember: People are reading your blog for information. If you know what you are talking about, they NEED your advice, and so a recommendation is actually helping them. Again, however, I repeat: Be honest and accurate. You never want to recommend a product you don't believe in.

With this end goal in mind then, let's look at some tips on how to figure out your site's most profitable keywords.

Getting Great Keywords

It's not rocket science to figure out what the keywords are for a site – but that doesn't mean everyone is doing it (or doing it well). So you can stand out by remembering a few guidelines:

• First, try to distill what your site is. If you can't describe your site adequately in 20 words or less, then you might be doing too many things. Look for lots of commas, ands, and ors in your description, which tell you you're trying to list too many things, and cover too much territory. In business, the "elevator pitch" is all about short descriptions, so can you describe your site's business in the time it takes to ride an elevator?

• Use jargon where required. If you are selling "Linux router software", don't just use simple keywords like "connect to the Internet", since people who use Linux are well aware of the jargon, and likely to search on those actual products and technical terms. Therefore you should use the terms they use. Likewise, if you're selling seeds, use the words people who buy them use. So what if others don't understand; you need to reach buyers first, and afterward you can always write articles for those other people to see if they're a buying market.

• Psychology is vital. Imagine you're a visitor, and you type in "sleep deprivation". What are you looking for? Information perhaps. But if you type in "sleep deprivation aids" you're likely looking for solutions – and possibly prepared to pay for them.

• Have a goal. Generally, a site is about making money. In some cases, that means getting people to sign up for information now, and selling to them later; in other cases, it's about making an immediate sale. Each of these involves using different ways to attract customers, both information oriented and sales oriented (remember those long and short search phrases?) Making and keeping a goal will help you focus on what you want exactly, and what keywords you'll use.

• Brainstorm. I say "sleep deprivation aids", and someone else says "how do I get a good night's sleep?" Completely different phrases – but the same end result. For this reason, it pays to spend some time thinking about keywords (and even checking with others) in order to get as many variations as practical.

So we have our focus and our niche. Now we need the best keywords. How? By thinking like our ideal visitor.

The Searcher Mindset

To narrow down those potential visitors, and get our ideal ones (the ones that will benefit us) we need to understand what their searches mean.

For example, not everyone is searching for the same thing, even if they use the same words. When I type in "sleep deprivation" for instance, I could mean:

• I've heard of the term, and want to know more about it; for instance, students doing a report. This person will likely go directly to Wikipedia, and buy nothing.

• I want to know more of the causes; someone wanting to help a friend, perhaps.

• I'm tired, and I'd like a solution for sleeping better. Our ideal customer, ready to click and look for solutions, possibly paying right away for them!

And that's just a few possibilities, so how can you know?

One solution is keyword research tools. Many sites out there will tell you (often for a fee) how often people search for specific terms. Google itself has a tool for keyword research (once available for all, it's now only available to Google advertisers). Using these you can create large lists of words people use in searches, and get a feel for what ones apply to your site. Ultimately, you might want to explore one of these (pricier) options to squeeze out the most from your site's potential search engine traffic.

However, when starting out., keywords don't have to be difficult. The solution is to think "long tail" – a fancy term for longer, more specific phrases (also called "more targeted" in the SEO world). For example, we saw that "sleep deprivation" could mean several things, but what do YOU want it to mean? In our example, we offer "solutions for sleep deprivation" and "ways to avoid sleep deprivation". Now the longer phrase is more exact for our customer.

From there, play searcher. Type these phrases in, and see what results Google gives you. What alternative words are suggested, what web pages results are displayed, and so on. Using a few simple searches like this will give you a tremendous amount of insight into what phrases your site should display.

Working with this, you'll soon have a solid list of search terms; together, they form a niche group, the words you'll focus on in your blog writing and keyword strategy. By looking up terms, and picking the ones that are appropriate to your theme, you'll soon have a core of keywords suitable for your site, and from which you can build on.

The topic of keyword research is vast (and a quick search on the Internet for "keyword research" will give you even more on the subject), but this will get you started. Think how a visitor thinks, use the words they use, and you'll show up in the search engines for the topics they (and you) want. Then, you'll be well on your way to getting read!

Keywords, Keywords Everywhere – But Where Exactly?

You've got your research and your topic solidly in mind. Now where do you get the most bang for your buck, so to speak? That is, where should the keywords be on your site?

Obviously, your articles need them, and we'll look into writing your articles in more detail in the next chapter. But you need to remember that search engines are computer programs – and computers programs are very literal, and very dumb. So to know how to get our keywords out there, we need to think like a search engine.

When search engines come to your website (called 'spidering' your 'web' site – cute, huh?), they visit each page and load them, much like a visitor dropping by and using their browser. It will follow all the links on each page, and from there reach throughout your site. Think of a hyperactive kid clicking on all your web page links, and you get an idea what a spider is like. However, unlike a human, hyperactive or otherwise, they do it systematically, automatically, and file it all away without comprehending the results.

For example, imagine a search engine loading in the pages of your website. It can't see, so the colors and images mean nothing to it. This can cause big problems:

• What if our sleep site has a picture of a person sleeping soundly as the logo. It may grab people, but the search engine won't give you any higher rankings for it.

• Likewise, your color scheme, cute layout, and inviting graphics: They may promote readability and keep visitors around a little longer, but none of this is noticed or factored in by the search engine spiders.

• Videos, like images, suffer from being 'opaque' to search engines, and require supplementary text to 'explain' them.

• JavaScript must be used cautiously. Although in recent years Google has stated it can scan web pages like a browser can (including JavaScript), on occasion it's missed bits and pieces. So if you use JavaScript for links or to generate content, try not to rely too much on the results getting indexed, just in case the search engines flub it.

OK, Google and Bing and any others can ignore big chunks of your site if you're not careful. What's left?

Words – because search engines LOVE text.

So obviously the goal is to get that text (and in particular, those valuable keywords) into your website in the best places.

Here's some ways:

• For the problem items, we add text around it. Just as JavaScript needs extra non–programming text to be safely used for links, so too we can introduce our Flash movies using text with concrete keywords, and we can add to our website logo with a slogan ("We help with sleep deprivation" in text right beside that nice sleepy person in the image, for instance).

• For other items, HTML provide tags we can use for adding keywords. In fact, good clean HTML (or XHTML, strictly speaking) must include text alternatives for images. These entries in XHTML are called the "title" and "alt" attributes, and are great for adding keywords. Now with that image of a tired person, not only can we put text beside the image, but we can include it in the `<img>` itself (underlined parts):

```
<img href="http://egwebsite.com/sleepy.jpg" title="solutions for sleeping
    problems" alt="Man with sleeping problems">
```

This extra text appears on several occasions: The `alt` text appears in place of the image if it's missing or not loaded (some people like to browse without loading images to speed things up); if you move your mouse over the image the `text` section should display in a popup (obviously, on a desktop computer!); or, if you happen to be a search engine spider robot, it's ALL available for search engine results!

• HTML tags can help focus the rest of the website. As we saw in the last chapter with themes, HTML tags like `<h1>` and `<h2>` help out the search engines by pointing them to important text. Your theme should handle these properly (including using good keywords there) to manage correct emphasis on your site.

• Finally, web pages also give hidden areas for keywords. In web pages, they include the `<title>` tag (which shows on the top bar of your browser, regardless of what text you have on screen), the `meta keywords` entry, and the `meta description` entry, two tags to add extra keywords and descriptive text, respectively.

We'll focus on this last group first, and see in the next section how we can manage better `<title>` and meta tags in our blog.

Those Invisible (But Useful) Tags On Your Web Page

To view these unseen entries, just go to your browser and visit any website. Then use the view source option (In FireFox or Chrome, right-click the window and select 'View Page Source'; other browsers are similar, or may have an option in their menu). You'll be looking at a text only version of the web page, the actual HTML/XHMTL that comprises it. There, near the top, you might see some entries:

```
<title>My Web Page Title - Visible In The Browser Window Frame</title>
<meta name="description" content="A blurb to describe the web page appears
    here" />
<meta name="keywords" content="blog,blogs,blogz,web page" />
```

The `meta description` and `meta keywords` entries are optional, and may not appear on every page; in contrast, the `<title>` tag is certain to be on every web page.

These can give SEO benefits if done right: Google (among others) will use the `<title>` tag for the title of their search engine entry. For this reason, you'll want to make sure the web page <title> tag is keyword friendly. And the meta description tag can provide extra text used by search engines, and possibly be the text displayed for the search engine result. If you've ever had trouble finding the actual text you read in a search listing on the website itself, it's possible a hidden tag like this was where the text was buried.

What about the third item, meta keywords? In the past, many have recommended this for extra keywords and word misspellings. After all, if Google only sees the keyword "caviar" on the site, will it understand that people also type in "fish eggs" or misspell it "cavier"? The keywords section was where you covered your bases.

Unfortunately, it seems that search engine use of it has dropped off. As far as the meta keywords tag goes, Google doesn't use it, and Bing states there's only 'some' benefit to it (search on "bing meta keywords" to read more of their views). Given the poor support for it, it doesn't seem worth the effort to maintain a barely–utilized tag, especially when your time can be better spent elsewhere improving your SEO. So avoid the meta keywords tag, and concentrate on a good description and web page title instead.

In the plugins chapter, we explained how to install the SEO plugin from Yoast. Now we'll explore how to use it for improved search engine value, providing the features that WordPress sorely lacks: A keyword–rich <title> tag and meta description tag.

The benefits? By default, WordPress has no meta description entry in the header. As well, it also improves the <title> tag, since your typical (default) home page entry might look like this:

```
<title>My Blog Title | Just another WordPress site</title>
```

Now if your blog is about sleep deprivation, and you've titled your blog "Sleep Deprivation Blog" followed by the article title, then you might be doing fine, with lots of good keywords in the <title>. However, there's some points to note:

• Few people have a blog title that fits in with their theme, keyword wise. In addition, as this example shows, adding 'blog' makes sense to visitors, but has little search engine benefit (unless you really want to be known as a blog on the topic, as opposed to just an information website, for instance). So what may be good for the blog's title is bad for the SEO <title>.

• With many themes, on all non–Home web pages the article or web page title comes first, followed by the blog title. This is good for SEO in that we tend to place emphasis on the first things (article title) rather than the second (blog title), and search engines reflect that (at least in English). However, you're still stuck with the blog title, which may not be as keyword–rich as you'd like.

• Each article in turn has a unique focus. A `<title>` entry, including the article's title, will help (if the article title is keyword-rich of course) but we can also add a summary of the article and have it appear in the `meta` `description`, giving us more search keywords in play.

That's the idea behind SEO. Using Yoast's plugin, We'll look at setting these two items up. In the process, you'll get an idea of how web page SEO works.

Using Yoast

We've already explained how to install the plugin and set it up. Once it's running, we'll visit two sections. The first is for post title usage. Go to **SEO; SEARCH APPEARANCE**, then the **CONTENT TYPES** tab. Farther down is the entry **SEO TITLE**, with the entries:

```
(Title) (Page) (Separator) (Site title)
```

In this case (the default) the blog post for a page on turtles might look like this:

```
My Painted Turtle 2 - Turtles Galore!
```

Of course, you can guess what the article title and the blog title are from this. And for every blog post, the `<title>` entry will change appropriately. So all done, right?

Usually. But let's say your blog is titled "Dave's Site" - what benefit is the site title then? So if you remove that tag from the **SEO TITLE**, then its shorter, and the keywords are more focused.

What if the post title is not keyword-rich? First off, you should redo your post title! It's too important to not have good keywords in it. But if you're still worried, you can add another tag here (via "Insert Snippet"), one for "Primary Category". And if the Category is a good keyword (and it should be) it can have the benefit of adding more keywords to the `<title>` entry.

Now, the description. Here, we go to individual posts via editing. On the edit page will be an entry for Yoast, including an entry "Meta Description". Just type here to add it to the `meta` `description` tag.

What to write? Imagine someone sees your post on Google – what summary will get them clicking through? Distill is down to just a few words, and make it a powerful teaser.

For example, the "My Painted Turtles" article will likely appeal to turtles fans in general – but which group do you really want to click? Is the article selling turtles, or vacations to view turtles, or even painted turtle soup (if such a thing exists?) The title gives some detail, but now the description can explain, focus more, and get exactly the traffic you want. With practice you'll find it easier to summarize articles, and benefit from that search engine exposure.

Summary

Yoast SEO handles much of the remaining SEO you'll need on your site. This section only touched briefly on what you can do with it – it's worthwhile to visit their site and see if any other features will help you in promoting your blog.

Of course, with a plugin like this, much is optional. You are actually doing quite well right after its install, so you only need to tweak as you learn. And with a plugin as popular as this, there are a lot of configuration articles on the Internet, so you can adjust settings slowly, and increase the benefits to your blog site as you get more comfortable with SEO.

The world of SEO is a vast one, and you can spend many hours (and many dollars) learning what works and what doesn't. For the price of this book, you now know the 90% that matters most: Keywords and keyword visibility. Focus on those items, and your websites have a much better chance of ranking high!

Remember The Lifeblood Of Any Website: Content!

I remember learning to use a typewriter in school (it was either that or learn French). For those who haven't typed on one, imagine your computer's word processor worked line by line (and you had to move the line back into place by hand!), and every correction used a lot of whiteout (and if you don't know what whiteout is, you're not missing much).

Plus, the result was one font only, no bold, no italic, and the font was always, well, typewriter font, mono–spaced and usually quite ugly.

Now, imagine using THAT to write!

Surprisingly enough, even with a clunker like a mechanical typewriter, people wrote – and wrote well. For about 100 years, typewriters provided a boon to writers everywhere; after all, before that it was all written by hand!

My point in bringing this up is that today's tools have made writing much easier, so much so that we can consider putting really large amounts of content onto a website as something practical.

It's true that typing speeds are about the same now as in the past. But the typewriter provided printed text only, so it still needed to be converted into another format for use, such as the printing plates needed to make a newspaper; and that took time. In contrast, when we type something today, it's ready to go – for the web, to print out, to email – and all with very little extra effort. Even proofreading is faster: I now have a program that highlights my spelling mistakes with little red underlines, saving me from consulting my pocket dictionary frequently (and that's only if I felt a word was misspelled, which meant I used to miss a lot of words!)

So with our enhanced productivity, how best to use it? In a nutshell, by creating lots of articles fast, and making sure the articles both draw in search engines, and please visitors. In fact, this prolific writing has become so common it's gotten a generic (and for a writer, somewhat disrespectful) title – content.

Nonetheless, the goal is producing article after article to fill up your website. And of course, these articles do need to be filled with valuable information. So then, how do I write lots and lots of quality articles and other 'content' that pleases search engines and humans alike? How exactly do my words help 'conquer' my niche?

As the last chapter pointed out, keywords are vital. But you need more: You need to write those keywords in such a way that search engines can target your site correctly, yet humans can still read the resulting articles.

After all, who hasn't seen a website article like this:

> *Looking for Q1U microphone from Samsung? The Q1U microphone from Samsung is a useful microphone. With lovely styling, the Q1U microphone from Samsung will be perfect anywhere. And...*

An article like this is obviously keyword driven, and utterly useless to people looking for information. Yet you see them from time to time because they work – sort of.

A search engine will come check it out, and see "Q1U microphone from Samsung" several times. It indexes it, and possibly ranks it high for the term. So, they likely get a search result.

But before you run out and write like this, consider the next step: Even if the search engine should rank it high, it's people that matter. And when they click, they'll look at the page, get mad, and leave the site immediately. No time on the site equals no time to sell, or otherwise make money. So the article did little real good.

Another factor to consider when writing is that search engines are in business – and their business is providing good results when you search. After all, if you don't get good listings, you can try another search engine, right? So search engines go out of their way to make sure their results are always worthwhile to the searcher (or as worthwhile as they can make them). This means they track things like clicks on their results, and also monitor sites. Plus, if you have a problem with a site, you can complain. And a direct complaint about any bad website is sure to make any search engine pay attention.

The result is that poor copy like this might work for a while; but search engines eventually catch on, and so it's a poor foundation to build a site on.

Instead of a mindless repetition of keyword phrases then, how about some variety – and more importantly, real information for the real people out there:

> *Looking for the Q1U microphone from Samsung? The Samsung Q1U USB powered microphone is a high quality audio microphone, yet plugs into your computer's USB port, and does not need batteries. Ideal for audio recording and editing, or even for producing podcasts, the Q1U USB powered microphone from Samsung is a perfect choice, yet inexpensive. And...*

Still a bit repetitive, but notice there is real information in these sentences. Additionally, people have more to search on. If I'm looking for a USB microphone, the before and after examples of this page might both be offered to me in my search engine results. But there's other searches the first example would not be part of, but this second one might:

```
podcast microphone
audio recording microphone
inexpensive computer microphone
```

Now, our content is readable for humans, yet still keyword–rich for computers. And in addition, it has a real purpose, and provides useful information.

So, quality content is vital to make your site work. But another aspect is focus, how the article fits in with your site overall.

Focus Your Articles

How does my blog focus affect what I write? Simply put, if you go off topic, search engines won't give you a break. We talked briefly about this already, but let's look at an example:

Your site is an authority on gerbils. Every page extolls the virtues of gerbils, and gives detailed discussions on gerbil–related information: Raising, caring, feeding, training, displaying.

You get the idea.

Now imagine posting one day about a sunset you saw on your way to work. Where do you think that post will end up in the search engines? The first page? Second?

Page 5,000?

Now, there are exceptions (you could have seen the sunset with the American President for instance, and people visit to find out about that), but generally, the site's focus determines how 'powerful' each article is. Stay in focus, and the articles will add to your site, building reputation and SEO.

Now, many people like to get very specific about content creation, citing keyword ratios and 'rules' about length and size. However, it's difficult to be very specific on what search engines like, and that's for a very specific reason: They'll never tell you how they work!

Search engines like to keep everyone in the dark, because if they spelled out exactly how they measured pages, then people would write precisely what the search engines want, and only that. In the end, everything on the Internet would be like our first microphone web page – SEO crap, with lots of keywords, yet little meaning, because 'meaning' has no meaning to a search engine spider.

So they keep us in the dark. And as we puzzle out what works, some get a bit caught up in the details. We know that content works, and that keywords work; but when people start discussing ratios and lengths and things of that nature, it starts moving into guesswork. And you can often avoid that with just a little common sense.

How Long Should Your Article Be?

Take for instance article length. The experts all agree – to disagree. An article can be 200 words. Or 400. Or 700. Or whatever people in that industry expect. And so on.

Yet if you go to the search engines, and do some checking, you'll find any type of article works: Long, short, you name it. So what length should your articles be?

Whatever it takes to get the job done.

And keyword ratios? Like the microphone articles, it's possible to jam lots and lots of keywords into a small space (called keyword stuffing). This stuffing increases the percentage of keyword content per article, called raising the keyword density. But, experts disagree on what density is best!

However, the fact is that search engines allow all kinds of articles on their first pages – low density, high density, and in between. Of course, there are extremes: If there are no specific keywords on the page, the search engines can't just make them up! Likewise, if the whole article is full of keywords and little else, the search engines will soon figure out how uninteresting the article is to people, and 'reward' the site with poor rankings. As with the length, the density should be whatever it takes to get the job done. But the article must be readable by humans AND readable by computers, so you need to balance interesting text with keyword–rich text.

Here's the good news: Keep your articles a reasonable length, use appropriate keywords, and search engines WILL help you out in their search engine listings. After all, their goal is to index all the relevant pages on each and every conceivable topic, and that means pages done by anyone, from poor struggling writers to professional SEO experts. As long as the page has valuable information, search engines want to show it to people.

But if you still feel there needs to be a guideline, try this: For the topic you are interested in, do some online searching, and see what the topmost pages are like. You'll find (with the few exceptions of people trying to 'game' the system, and possibly not being there for long), that pages are approximately 300–700 words, keyword–rich, and informative. So you must write the same!

This also applies to tone and style of writing. You've read government guides, the type of weird speech that only government guide writers use. However, if you were marketing to government guide writers ("A Government Guide Writer's Guide To Writing Government Guides", perhaps?) then you'd do well to have the same tone and style.

Write the way your market expects, or expect to not reach that market!

A Short Guide To WordPress Article Writing

Now in WordPress, you have an easy time of writing; simply click on **Posts**; **Add New** via the Admin menu and write away. Or like I've mentioned, write locally, polish your words, and then copy and paste them into the WordPress edit box for a new post.

Once you hit **Publish**, you're good to go, right?

Well, yes – but with a bit of tweaking, you can get a whole lot more bang for your buck!

That's because the article itself is only one part of the text the blog presents to search engines. In a very rough order of importance, here is what makes a search engine happy:

• Keywords in the URL (the slug, or permalink). The post URL is visible in search engine listings, and keywords there are a great way to add to the SEO reach of the article (Hint: It's also a great way to place keyword misspellings into an article listing, like 'suduku' instead of 'sudoku').

• Optimized `<title>` tag. As already discussed, a `<title>` tag that focuses on the article title instead of the blog title is a good idea. For many search engine results this will become the title of the listing, so making the `<title>` entry as effective as possible is probably the single biggest benefit from using an SEO plugin.

• A good article title. Obviously, if the `<title>` tag is set up to display your post's title, then the post title itself had better be inviting and keyword–rich. After all, when people search on "how to build a patio", they are more likely to be delivered (and then click on) a page whose title is also "how to build a patio", what they asked for. So keywords count here big time, both for SEO and people.

• Good `meta description` text. For some search engine results, this description is what is actually displayed. A keyword–rich one helps with indexing, while a well–written one invites people to click through to the site. If you're using a plugin that displays the `meta description` text for each post, seriously consider using it.

• A good first paragraph. It's part psychology, part search engine workings, but search engines (and people) tend to focus on the front of a web page, much like we do, and text buried near the bottom of an article is considered less important. So it's vital to get the information (and keywords, and the 'hook') out there as soon as possible.

When writing, take a cue from newspaper reporters. They've been taught to 'lead' with the story, putting the most important details early in the article, and the least important ones later on. That way, the end could be trimmed off to fit without losing the most valuable parts of the story. Newspapers are the original disposable media, and they work hard to get readers; you can learn a lot from their style.

• A good article. Like newspapers, every paragraph should count. Ramble on for a few thousand words, and your keyword ratio will naturally drop. Worse yet, readers will get bored and give up, always a bad thing. So say what you need to, and then stop. Likewise, if the topic is naturally going on for too long, consider splitting it into separate articles. You'll get better focus for each of the resulting articles, and as an extra benefit, you'll end up with more web pages!

• Keywords in images or media. Using `alt` or `title` attributes for images are helpful for people not seeing them (either due to disabilities or having image viewing turned off), and they also provide extra fodder for search engines, if the text is keyword–rich.

This is of course only a partial and incomplete list of what search engines like. There are many, many other factors search engines can use to decide rankings, and many of which they will never reveal to us to prevent 'gaming' or 'fixing' of websites unfairly. Nonetheless, these are valuable factors in your web page standings; try to include most of them, and you are well on your way to writing articles that make search engines happy!

Combined with the site–wide tweaks we've talked about earlier, like making category names keyword–rich, or adding `alt` and `title` attributes to header and footer images, you get a twofold benefit: The website as a whole has keywords that help focus it, and each article's specific keywords can both add to those, and at the same time branch out into a new topic (but on the same theme of course). Together, you maximize search engine range and reach.

OK, following these tricks puts a smile on Google's face – now what about people? That's where you need to add a little more psychology to your writing...

Writing For Man, Or Machine?

Should you write for people or for machines?

The fact, is, you must do both!

Without the keyword–oriented articles, search engines won't know where to place you, since keywords are how search engines connect searchers with valid results. After all, if you search on 'Nova', can you trust the search engine to understand you meant a car, and not an exploding star? And if you do mean a car, will it give you pages for the word 'car' as well? Or perhaps 'automobile'? That's pretty typical for a human, but asking a lot (maybe too much) from any search engine.

But even though humans are smarter, we're more fickle, too. Give us an article like our earlier example on the Q1U microphone, and we get annoyed – and rightly so.

That means our keyword–rich web page also has to be interesting. But what does that mean exactly?

In a nutshell:

The article must accomplish the goal of the article.

Very Zen–like I know, but think of it: If you write an article reviewing the Q1U microphone, what is a visitor to expect? A review of the microphone, no more, no less. But I once went to a page on building a wooden stand, and instead of the expected how–to guide, the article talked about a project the author might do someday. All the right keywords were there, so the article was indexed and found by me – but the page was a placeholder, with no real information. Very irritating!

And as we saw, the title of the article helps a lot in the search engine indexing, so your title also needs to match the article. Therefore, if your title promises something, make sure your article delivers exactly that – or change your title!

How To Write A Money–Making Article

However, there's more to writing than just typing away on any subject. Unless you're a blogger working to sell your words as a book, more than likely you'll want money (directly) from your words. After all, if you've written a review of the Q1U microphone, wouldn't a few ads for the product around that blog post be handy? So then someone comes to your review, reads about how good the product is, and there you are with a link to purchase right now. The perfect impulse buy, and a commission for you, the helpful author.

While that's not the way every sale will go (I doubt a car review site would profit from "buy now" style cars ads!), it does mean that your articles should target your money–making goals:

• Include a call to action. By the end of the article, tell them what they should do. If the review is positive, tell them they will benefit from buying it; if the review is bad, suggest better ones (and make sure those reviews are on your site ASAP). Guide your visitors to what will profit you most – like the ads.

• Be honest and trustworthy. You can inform people, but be careful to never lie or mislead. If a product is bad, trying to sell people on it will come back to haunt you later on, destroying your online credibility.

• Don't be complete. I've mentioned this trick since my earliest guides: If your goal is to send them somewhere, never COMPLETELY explain everything! For instance, if you talk about podcasting with microphones, you can go into some detail, but don't worry about writing the ultimate podcasting guide. As a result, when they reach the article end, and they see an ad for further podcasting information (you are using ads, aren't you?), they might click on it. And that click profits you precisely because you aren't trying to answer every question they have right there and then.

• Use the appropriate language and terms. We've discussed this in keywords already, but it's important to remember that if people look for a technical term, that term must be in the article. And if your market doesn't use that term, then make sure the ones they do search for are found there.

Also, remember that different markets have different terms, and your article should use the words appropriate to your audience, to help with familiarity. After all, cake manufacturers and cake eaters use different words to describe the same thing: "Mouth feel" versus "luscious", "sugar" or "sweet" versus "high fructose corn syrup", and so forth. Use the right terms, and you'll come across as an 'insider', and therefore more credible (and more likely to make a sale). So depending on whom you're reaching in each article, you'll need to use the appropriate vocabulary.

Focus your article, target it to your market, make it satisfying (but not too satisfying), and write it not too short yet not too long. Have we covered everything?

Just about – we also need to cover how often to write.

How Often Should You Publish?

The reasons to write often are simple: Search engines and people.

Imagine you're a search engine. You visit a site, and nothing changes. You come back in a week and still nothing is different. But you're a busy search engine spider with places to go and websites to see, so what do you do? Simply make a note not to visit too often.

But imagine that same spider dropping by and the website has changed. Now it says "Oh no, I'm missing valuable information my masters need to serve accurate and worthwhile content to their human clients" (spiders are somewhat verbose that way). So the spider makes a note to come back soon, sooner than if there were no changes. And then it comes back faster and faster if the information changes quickly enough –

after all, just look at how fast news articles are indexed on large sites like CNN or BBC News.

On the other hand, people have lives, and a new blog post every 15 minutes means most of them are going unread. And if you're like me, knowing you always have to catch up on your blog reading is a sure way to get the site dropped entirely from your to–do list. Yet they have to write something from time to time, or else why should I bother visiting? (Of course I realize that in the world of Twitter, Instagram, and Facebook there is a case to be made for very frequent updates. But their 'post' size is smaller than most blog posts are; and even with those sites, there's a limit as to how frequently you should add content).

So search engines want frequent updates, and people want it more leisurely. Who wins?

You need a compromise. Many bloggers post daily. But few popular bloggers post less than weekly. So my minimum recommendation has been to write daily for a month or so when you start out with your blog, and then taper back. But always try to get at least a post or two out there each week. The result is your site changes, and the spiders have a reason to keep coming back frequently.

And of course, you can write much more often. I personally find it excessive to read more than a couple of posts a day on a blog, but that's me. After all, look at Twitter – people can read huge numbers of posts a day from some of the more popular Twitterers. Also, Facebook and Instagram updates can suck up huge amounts of the day for some people. And in fact many popular bloggers write more like two or three posts a day, so if you have the stamina for it, go ahead, you won't break anything in the search engines!

However, it's easy to SAY write every day, but it's another thing to go and do it consistently. If you read a lot of blogs out there, you'll soon see the same pattern; many start strong, but eventually daily becomes weekly, then monthly, then never again – and that can all happen quickly.

So plan for it. Expect to write frequently at first, and then have it taper off in time. But try to set a goal to never get below a weekly posting or two.

Moreover, like dieting, don't give up. Even if you ignore your blog for a month or so, just start writing again. It might take a while, but you will get more frequent spider visits, and your posts will again make it into the search engine results fast.

Now to round out the topic of content writing, how about some technical tips for your blog?

The WordPress Content–Booster Trick

You've written a great 1,500 word article, and don't feel like rewriting it into three 500 word articles. Not all is lost: Here's a trick to make that article do triple duty with very little effort.

Go to the WordPress Admin **POST EDIT** page for that article, and add this little text command:

```
<!--nextpage-->
```

In WordPress, you can insert this code anywhere in the text to split the pages (be sure the editor is in Text mode, so that this text is recognized by WordPress as an HTML command). When the blog displays the final article, it will break it up into two pages. Add another entry, and it will break it into three pages, and so on.

Instant extra content!

The result is you get more pages for search engines, and more pages for readers (and more ads if you're using them). Plus you have more focused pages, since a whole article might discuss several topics, but the resulting sections are more narrowly targeted, and therefore ideal for search engines.

One problem with this trick is that not all WordPress themes handle it properly. To check if your theme does so, add an article to your site, split it up, and then view the post on your blog. If you can navigate from page one to page two without problems, then your theme is fine, and search engines should have no trouble either. If not, you might wish to go with another theme.

Crafting Links In Your Articles

Another trick is for handling article links effectively.

Frequently, you'll want to link to another site, so a typical link might look like this in your article (via the Text editor of course; in the Visual editor you'll get the blue link underline instead):

```
<a href="http://egwebsite.com/page1">
```

But if you change the link to this:

```
<a href="http://egwebsite.com/page1" target="_blank">
```

You'll now open a new browser window when you click on the link, leaving the original window, with your blog page, intact. While annoying for some people, the benefit is that your site is still in the browser, and therefore people don't leave, never to come back. Of course, they can still leave, but they'll need to go through the extra step of closing that original window.

Note that you can also do this semi-automatically. In the Text editor, highlight a section of text, and then click on the link button "<u>link</u>" just above the editor. A popup appears where you can enter the link (URL) and includes the checkbox "Open link in a new tab". Check this to add the `target="_blank"` without typing it in.

Now to close off this chapter on content and writing, one touchy subject – writing and the law.

Legal No–Nos

As the final point about writing, there's always the legal aspect of anything you put in print. Remember:

• Libel is bad.

• Plagiarism is bad.

• Trademark infringement is bad.

It's easy to say something online that goes too far, and with the legal system the way it is worldwide, you could actually get yourself in trouble with a very small comment. After all, why do coffee cups at restaurants now warn us that their contents are hot?

Whether you did anything wrong or not, and whether a legal claim is frivolous or not, lawyers are expensive; so avoid defaming anyone online. Even a celebrity might take exception, and while not likely, do you (and your pocketbook) want to chance it?

As for copyright, that's even worse. Stealing someone's article or content, or even thinly tweaking it to look like your own, is a huge fine: In the United States for example, copyright infringement can cost you upwards of $150,000! So until you get your law degree, the best option is to do all your own research, and write everything in your own words. It's more work, but you avoid nasty legal bills.

Lastly, trademark infringement: I get really annoyed every time I see a domain URL with the word "WordPress" in it (except for the main WordPress sites, of course). The reason is that WordPress Central is now legally obligated to fight that trademark infringement, costing them time and money.

As well, people who set up sites like that invest a lot in a website that WILL be taken away from them when they are successful. The reason is simple: If the owner of the WordPress trademark doesn't fight back, then the trademark can become generic and usable by all, much as 'aspirin' has ceased to be a trademarked name. It's called dilution of trademark, and it's a real problem particularly when a competing site becomes well known and potentially confusing. So small sites may get ignored for a while, and then hit when they finally reach the big time – and when they least want it to happen.

What does this mean? If you feel like putting 'eBay', 'Google', or 'WordPress' in your domain name, avoid the temptation. And make it clear when you write that trademarked names are trademarked. For example, the owners of the Kleenex trademark post notices in magazines warning writers to avoid using it as a generic term, to prevent diluting it ("she used a Kleenex tissue" instead of "she used a Kleenex"). For all trademarked terms in your writing, that's a good idea.

Fortunately, if you take a bit of care in your writing, legal issues should be no problem. And if you also take care to make sure your words are well written both for the search engines and people, you can expect good results not only with those search engines, but also when real live searchers drop by for a visit.

You NEED Traffic To Your Site (And Here's How To Get It)

Location, location, location – it's the mantra of real estate people everywhere. Especially when it's a location for business.

There's a mall not far from where I live, and it constantly changes stores inside. But the odd thing is that the turnover is mainly in one section of the mall; there, shops try and try and try, yet keep failing.

Of course, it's no real surprise if you know one more detail: The failing businesses are all on the lowest level at one end, and all depend on casual traffic to survive. Where they are located, fewer people stroll by, and so they end up with less potential customers. And no customers means no business. In contrast, the Optometrist next door doesn't need as much walk–in traffic (they have repeat clients), so they've stayed there successfully for years.

My mall isn't unique of course, since location affects every business. But here's the rub: Online, there is no 'here', and every site is as easy to get to as any other site. Online, the physical location of your website isn't the issue, since it's likely in some unknown server computer thousands of miles away, just like everyone else.

Yet if location isn't the same for online businesses, is there something else that IS just as vital for them as a good 'location' is for real–world shops?

"Location, Location, Location" For The Internet

To understand this, think of a restaurant. Now, in the real world (sometimes called "offline" or "bricks and mortar"), a restaurant needs a good location. Some restaurants can get ahead with an out of the way place, but then the reviews have to be spectacular, or word of mouth really, really good; after all, few people are going to

---

drive way across town for just any restaurant!

So the key to the restaurant's success is to be connected to people in some way: Close by where they live or work, well reviewed, or recommended by friends. Otherwise, it likely won't survive.

And online? Sites need to be connected too. And while we see that physical location isn't important, the remaining two are both forms of links: Links from reviews, or recommendation links from friends. Someone has to tell us if the restaurant is worth a visit, and someone has to tell us the same for that new website, too.

That's how it is online. There are many, many sites, so we need someone to spell out where to find them, and if they are any good. Mostly, that's the job of the search engines. But there are other sites that can help us as well. They work on the basis of friends helping friends, or social networking. After all, when you want a good restaurant, do you check a generic list like a phone book, or ask a few friends?

The result is simple – you need links to get your site out there. Links from search engines, links from other sites, or even paid links. Because without those links to your site, you will struggle for traffic.

Finding Your "Links" To Success

This section talks about getting links to your website. We've already explained how pinging and well–written articles (along with SEO formatted web pages and good keywords) can help the search engines link to you properly. So since we've focused on search engine linking, let's now see how we can get links from other places (and people).

There are many benefits from getting those extra links:

• You can never get enough good links. Links are a measure of site popularity, and search engines take this into account when they rank you. That is, all other things being equal, a site with 1,000 good links pointing to it will do better that one with 100.

Note here that I said "all things being equal" and "good links". The search engines rate links to your site, and there are many factors involved in these ratings, so 1,000 and 100 may not be uneven after all in the real world (of course, more is a good direction to go in).

For example, it's possible to get links to your site from bad neighborhoods, sites that search engines have a low opinion of, for example sites that sell links purely to 'game' the search engines. These types of links are risky, since if the search engine feels you're trying to get links artificially, it can penalize your site. Think of it this way: A shady–looking guy from a bad part of town recommends your restaurant. Is that 'link' worthwhile? How many real visitors will it bring? Not as much as a glowing 'link' from a local newspaper or television reviewer!

• Not everyone uses search engines to find things. For instance, my wife finds new blogs to read by checking links on blogs she likes, rather than the search engines. And look at eBay or any other large site: Who uses Google to search for an item there? So other kinds of links do matter.

• Links are read by people, and people are social. Like the restaurant example, a friend's recommendation can heavily influence you. And in the case of my wife, the links on the blogs she reads carry more weight than a random link she encounters elsewhere. They also carry implied trust; someone she approves of approved the link. So instead of checking the search engines, visiting the sites, and judging it herself, she can rely on the blogger to recommend the site. In fact, the term "social networking" refers to people connecting with people, and the extra impact a friend's recommendation can make. So links like that are quite valuable!

• Ironically, the quality of the links you get via search engines depends in large part on the links you get from other websites! By linking to you in the normal, unpaid–for fashion (also called linking 'organically'), search engines see these links and consider them like votes on the popularity of your site.

• Paid links can help you out by sending traffic from one site to another (yours). I know I said earlier paid links were a no–no with the search engines. They are, if their purpose is to trick the search engines by making your site look more popular that it is. Those links try to look natural to deceive the search engines, and if found out, can actually hurt you. In contrast, obvious paid links like advertising are fine, and a great way to send traffic to your site if you have the money.

> So how do sites show search engines that a paid link is not an attempt to cheat? Search engines have agreed on an HTML tag to indicate these links, called 'nofollow'. You add the phrase to an `<a>` link tag, as in this underlined portion:

```
<a href="http://egwebsite.com/" rel="nofollow">a link</a>
```

This tells the search engine the link is not natural, and should not be followed by them in the course of ranking each site for its search engine results (they CAN follow it if they wish, of course). If you look at the HTML code of comments on many blogs, you'll see this tag. In fact, it was because of blog comments that the nofollow entry was developed. Spammers were commenting heavily on blogs, hoping to get hundreds and thousands of real–looking links easily. It grew so bad that nofollow was invented so that they would get no search engine benefit, and to hopefully make them quit the practice. While they haven't given up completely, we now have a way of telling search engines a link is not a natural one that they should use for search engine ranking. For this reason, it's perfect for advertising links, which are targeted at humans, while allowing sites to keep search engines happy.

Linking Strategies – Money Or Honey?

So links from other sites are vital, and we want them – now how do we get them?

In getting links there are two choices, what I like to call "money or honey".

'Money', of course, refers to advertising links. You pay for ad space, and hopefully send viewers to your site.

'Honey' refers to putting something on your site that is attractive to others, and so they link to you naturally. Put a cute picture or YouTube video up, and people might link to it.

For both, the goal is simple: People come to visit that web page, and maybe stay to check the rest of the site out. In time, perhaps they buy something, or otherwise help promote your niche (like offer you a book deal or a consulting gig).

Both 'honey' and 'money' are vital to a thriving online business. We understand the SEO benefits of natural linking; as for business links, despite not giving you search engine 'juice', they do give you traffic, and traffic means sales. As well, the quality of the traffic can be better. After all, you call the shots on your ad, and what you want to feature, so the visitor is already interested in your product or service when they click. This kind of prefiltered traffic (called qualified or targeted traffic) is a great boon to your marketing efforts.

So let's just look at the different methods of promoting your site, and ways to get traffic there.

Traffic Method #1: Video

People are visual, and whether you like it or not, video rules the web. YouTube exploded from nothing in 2006 to being the powerhouse it is today because of video. And free video, no less.

However, a huge site like that has a problem: There are so many videos online now that wading through them is next to impossible. That's where blogs come in. A blog can cherry–pick the most relevant videos for that niche, add surrounding text on the page, and the combination of blog focus and video interest works together to help the site's rankings.

There are many websites that just add commentary to videos out there, and people appreciate it, especially if the topic stays focused (in other words, if you have a cat site, stay with cat videos if at all possible). But more than likely you're running a business, and videos mean a way to present your product. In that case, videos do double duty: Create a video showcasing your product, upload it to YouTube (with the extra traffic found there), and also place the video on your site.

Called embedding, each YouTube video includes code on its page that you can insert into a post, so to display it on your blog. For example, a YouTube embed code might look like this (remember to add this via the Text panel of the post editing window):

```
<object width="480" height-"385"><param name="movie"
    value="http://www.youtube.com/v/YEEksidloJzg4&amp;hl=en_US&amp;fs=1"></pa
    ram><param name="allowFullScreen" value="true"></param><param
    name="allowscriptaccess" value="always"></param><embed
    src="http://www.youtube.com/v/YEEksidloJzg4&amp;hl=en_US&amp;fs=1"
    type="application/x-shockwave-flash" allowscriptaccess="always"
    allowfullscreen="true" width="480" height="385"></embed></object>
```

You just paste the appropriate code into your post and publish. Of course, it's vital to add some keyword–rich text to the post so that the search engines have something to use in their indexing.

By the way, if you place your own videos on YouTube, make sure to link back to your site. While not every viewer will visit, make sure it's their choice, and not because they don't know where to go!

This also works for other video sites besides YouTube. And if it's a specialty video site (say, for how–to videos), you might get a more targeted audience by posting your videos there. But of course if you publish anything, consider submitting it to YouTube, as they are the king of online videos.

Traffic Method #2: Text Links

Despite video getting all the attention, we still use words; and words are vital for search engines, so text linking is still a great plan. As mentioned, you can pay for text links, and then there are organic text links. Now you shouldn't pay for the latter, but that doesn't mean you can't ask for them. One technique that works: Place a link on your site to another site, then email that site's owner to tell them about it. At the same time, ask for a reciprocal link, and wait. If you try this, remember that the email you send is important. It can't appear spammy; if I get a link request that looks like a machine wrote it, I don't even finish reading it, and neither will anyone else. Also, it must be relevant, so don't email a pet site for a link to your swimming pool website.

The format of the link is important, too. While you can't control the link words they'll end up using, you can suggest, and including a sample link (or offering a choice) might help. A typical link looks like this:

```
<a href="http://egwebsite.com/yourlink"
    title="sleep disorder assistance">sleep help</a>
```

Besides the visible text 'sleep help', you also have the `title` text you can use (here underlined). Adding it is a good idea, since search engines can give higher priority to the text in these links (which after all makes sense, since these links are a description of the destination page). If the other site uses the link as is, you get a bonus, with two pieces of SEO text in there. So make them readable for people, but don't forget those valuable keywords.

If they don't use the link within a few days, it's OK to email them one or two more times at most, politely of course. And if you don't hear from them, consider whether you'll remove their link from your website. You might decide to leave it; after all, as you try to get links from the best sites in your niche, those links going out could build up a "who's who" listing of the related sites out there. Eventually, you may find that you've become the information hub for people researching that niche, and in turn this could help your rankings.

Traffic Method #3: Paid Links

As I've said, I don't recommend paying for a link for search engine benefits since it could come back to haunt you. However, people do this regularly, and so you might wish to. In that case, find a site that is popular and high profile in your industry, and ask to place a paid link on it. If the website is well–known on this topic, search engines will take note of the link, and your site could benefit from their 'vote'.

> Stealth linking (links that are paid for, yet are made to look organic to the search engines, and lacking the `nofollow` attribute) is a controversial topic. Some marketers swear by paid links on specific websites for generating search engine rankings, since a link from the right site could mean a real boost. For example, if your site is on cats, imagine how a stealth link from a major cat site would help your rankings and traffic (of course you can also get the traffic, but without the rankings, using a paid non–stealth advertisement on their site). However, if it's found out, the search engines may penalize you. So before searching for paid links of this type, remember to evaluate the pros and cons.

For linking, there are different placements possible. In–article links can be very effective, since they look natural, and people are more inclined to see them and click on them. However, a site–wide link, such as in a sidebar, can be good, since it is visible across multiple pages. You'll pay more for the site–wide exposure, of course, but that extra exposure should make it worthwhile. So if you have a choice between a single page or many pages, go for the multiples; but if the choice is for a single link in an article or one near it (but not in it), go for the article link.

Traffic Method #4: Social Sites

On the subject of well–respected sites (also known as authority sites), one huge area for valuable traffic is social bookmarking. Search engines pay careful attention to social sites, and links on them get quick action. For example, you can promote a blog post on your Facebook page, handy if you have a lot of fans. Is it worthwhile overall? In every case, look at the sites first, and get an idea what is popular on them. If your posts are a good fit, it can pay for you to list your articles with them each time you post.

Social websites can be a boon for traffic because people are influenced greatly by friends and acquaintances, and so links on these sites have more impact. Also, because of the high traffic these sites receive, and their popularity, links there can often get great exposure.

Sites like FaceBook, LinkedIn, Instagram and Twitter give you an opportunity to get the word out. And while these sites have social aspects, even just setting up a member page of your own on any (or all of them) can give you a chance to add links; and these links can help your overall link building strategy.

Traffic Method #5: Writing

However, a link or two from your FaceBook page pales into insignificance compared to links from articles you write and post online.

Besides their own content, other sites can publish your content. If you can get a link included (and you should always get a link included) the result is that traffic on their site might be coerced into visiting your site.

There are some details to get right, however:

• Obviously, this method can be a lot of work, so you have to target the right sites. Their market must match yours; for example, if their site is knitting-oriented, and your site is heavy-metal oriented, don't expect big results!

• Make sure they will accept articles. Some groups (like Huffington Post) post submission guidelines; others do not, and you may have to contact the site owner to see if they are interested. And by the way, do not expect payment for writing; if you're hoping to be paid, you may find very few sites are interested (or even respond to your email).

• Articles must be original and your own. They must also be unique; that is, don't expect good results if you send the same article to site after site after site. However, if you rework the articles (rearrange and redo sentences and paragraphs, change words to synonyms, and so forth), then each article becomes unique, and more acceptable.

• Vital to success is that you have a powerful call to action in the bio, which usually appears at the end of the articles. When people get to the end, they should read it and immediately click to your site. To write a good call to action, always put yourself in the reader's mind: Why are they reading this, and what vital information can you offer them on your site that they MUST have?

• Most sites allow at least one link in the bio blurb (and if they don't allow any live links, avoid them). That link should never point to your home page. Instead, always point it to a special page for visitors who came from reading these articles. Remember, the reader has gotten to the end, their curiosity piqued by your bio, and they've clicked for more information. So now what else are they expecting? Give it to them exactly, and you improve your chances of success. Go in another direction, and they will too – right off your site!

More Traffic Methods

Another way to get free or inexpensive traffic is with Twitter. Possibly the ultimate social site, Twitter allows people to send and read short messages of 140 characters, about the length of a phone text message. That's not a coincidence, as Twitter was designed to work with your phone's texting, allowing you to send twitterings from anywhere.

Note that Twitter is good for traffic, but it's poor for linking. Due to the small spacing for messages, putting a direct link to your site in a message is unlikely, since most links need to be shortened using a link conversion service like `bit.ly`, which takes a long URL and change it into a short one, like http://bit.ly/2MpFwye

However, if you build up readers, then Twitter can be useful to get people to follow you and what you mention. This leads to affiliate linking, or promoting your website. With a large enough following, your options for money–making increase greatly. And while the subject of Twitter and making a success of it can fill a book (and does, several in fact), you can start right away to try it out. Simply join up for a free account and start posting; this way, you'll see if the time and effort involved is a good fit for you.

Besides Twitter, there are other popular ways to get traffic, such as:

• Forum postings. If you belong to (or join) a forum related to your blog's topic, then every post you make there can help you get viewed as an expert. Write well, provide valuable information, and you'll get maximum benefit. If allowed, edit your signature, that text appearing at the bottom of each of your posts. Usually you can place some call to action there, as well as a link to your site, encouraging people to visit.

• Email signatures. The signature trick also works with emails. Each email system is a little different, but all of them allow you to automatically add a text ending to each email. Like the forum posts, this can include live links to your site, a call to action, and even explain benefits for the viewer. Make it memorable and interesting, and you'll get clicks.

• Blog commenting. Reading an interesting blog on your site's topic? Then leave a comment, along with a link back to your site. This has the benefit of showing readers who you are and how you think – and the possibility of getting real, live readers to click through to your site.

Finally, no matter what the promotion method, remember that your chosen words tell a lot about you and your business, and can encourage visitors to drop by your website; they can also do the opposite. But in either case, your words will likely stay on the Internet a long, long time. Avoid arguments and fights online, be respectful, write carefully, and you'll find your words a powerful advertisement for your business!

Advertising Traffic

Many of the traffic generators we've covered so far are free or nearly free, unless you decide to hire someone to do the work for you, like writing articles or submitting your site to directories.

There are of course many paid traffic options available also. However, as they used to say, "you pays your money and you takes your chances". Especially when using a paid service, it's important to understand some math basics before you commit a lot of money. Simply put, you need to know how much you make from each customer, and how much it costs to acquire each customer. Otherwise, you'll never know if you're getting ahead, or falling behind!

For example, say you advertise an offer with the popular service Adwords, and spend $100. You get 30 people clicking through, and 5 buy. Of course, you'll have to know which of these buyers actually came via the ads; there are some more complicated ways, like using Google Analytics, but we'll assume for this example that you offered them a unique price that only they get; that will let you track the buyers.

So, the end result is each customer cost you:

```
$100 spent / 5 customers = $20 spent per customer
```

Note that the 30 who clicked are immaterial – it's the 5 who bought that count. If you sell your product for $50, and spent $20 in advertising, then you made a $30 profit on each sale – not bad. But if you instead sell your product for $15, and you take away the advertisement cost of $20 for each sale, then you have a loss per customer of $5. In other words, the ad isn't working well enough.

Of course, this doesn't take into account fixed costs like staff expenses, site maintenance costs, hosting, and so on, but it's a good start towards calculating how much your advertising is making you. Remember, you want positive results from ads. Even if they don't buy a product, there must be a profit – visitors alone mean nothing to the bottom line, unless they open their checkbooks.

The True Value Of A Subscriber

Of course, sometimes the math isn't easy. If you use Adwords to get people signed up to your website's newsletter, how do you price that? Unfortunately (and somewhat mercilessly), in Economics, a newsletter subscriber is considered valueless until they start spending.

However, with time you'll be able to figure out the actual value of a subscriber by calculating how much you earn from email offers to your own list, and dividing that by the list's total subscribers. For instance, if you make an average of $1,000 a month in sales advertising to your list of 10,000 people, then the list value is 10 cents per subscriber per month:

```
$1,000 sales per month / 10,000 members = $0.10 per subscriber per month
```

Now based on this, an advertising expense of $100 had best give you 1,000 new subscribers if you want a quick return on your investment:

```
$100 spent / $0.10 earned per member per month = 1,000 subscribers needed
```

Of course, that's for a one–time investment (one month). But with subscribers, you'll likely have them for months and months, buying regularly. So a subscriber that stays with you for 10 months might be expected to spend $1.00 overall on average (10 months x $0.10), and you'll only need to get 100 of those with your $100 Adwords budget to break even.

If instead the typical subscriber stays with you for 1 year, then the overall average value of that subscriber (called the "lifetime value") is 12 x $0.10, or $1.20, and the number of those you'll need is:

```
$100 spent / $1.20 subscriber lifetime value = 83.3 subscribers needed
```

Or about 84 new subscribers.

Of course, the actual value of a customer can be more than a single sale. They may refer you to their friends, purchase again regularly, and so on. So this lifetime value of a subscriber can only give you an approximate idea of how much you should spend on advertising. But using it can help you get "in the ballpark" with your advertising expenses.

That's more math than you'll likely need right away; however, your ultimate goal will be to understand what the value of your client, subscriber, or customer is, and not pay more than that for advertising. Businesses in the early 2000s threw money around, and hoped that customers would become more valuable over time. They didn't, and we reached the end of the first dot–com era. Make sure you're profitable from the beginning, and you'll avoid becoming a statistic like them!

Best Places To Advertise

You've done the math, you've figured the customers you'll need. Now how do you spend your money? There are lots of companies willing to take it, but here are some of the more popular (and reliable) ways for a beginner to trade money for traffic and clients:

• Adwords. Probably the premiere service out there, you select keywords relevant to your site, create an ad to get people to click, and publish it. The result is that within minutes you can get visitors to your site. This simplicity however hides a real problem: If you don't know what you're doing, it's easy to shoot yourself in the foot – and Adwords can be a very expensive gun! Before trying out Adwords, study as much as you can, and roll out ad campaigns slowly. Also, watch your money carefully. Almost everyone has a war story about the first time they used Adwords, and saw their whole budget disappear in no time at all.

However, despite these warnings, Adwords is a great way to get traffic to your site. Craft a good ad, send visitors to a part of your site ready to convert them, and you are well on your way to a profitable business.

• The other search engine ad companies. Adwords is the biggest one on the block, but it's not alone; others have their own competing ad services. However, unless you're an Adwords veteran looking for new markets to conquer, branching out is a lot of effort for much smaller gains. Google has a huge lead in market share with advertising, and far more exposure than all the others combined. Nonetheless, these can be another source of traffic if you need it, and on occasion cheaper.

• Facebook. Whole books can (and are) written about social media advertising. Key to Facebook advertising is understanding the market. Hard sells do not work well there, since people visit for socializing, not research (unlike Google, where a person is researching, and often hoping for a solution). Key also is imitating what others are successful with, and starting slow, expanding as you prove successful.

• Amazon. Another option, Amazon searchers are definitely looking for products! If you have a product, Amazon can be a good fit (for example, if you are an author looking to sell more copies of your books). Again, like all adverting, start small and carefully.

• Email services. I'm not referring to your own email service, which is discussed in the next chapter. This is using someone else's service; for example, paying for an ad in their newsletter, and gaining traffic that way.

Newsletter emailings have a spotty record, so spotty in fact that I recommend you only use this option on one condition: It's an ad in an email newsletter you read and enjoy. Your exposure to the newsletter will help you understand if the list is valuable, what they expect, how to write the ad for maximum benefit, and so forth. After all, if you don't read it, how can you expect anyone else to? For example, a newsletter you barely look at may be uninviting to most others as well. But the one you read immediately (and completely) each time it arrives – THAT'S the one you want to contact the list owner and discuss ad rates with!

• General emails ('spam'). I mention this because people do it, and it rarely goes over well. The first spam complaint I ever had was when I used an email service I thought was reputable. Make no mistake, you will be tempted: 1,000,000 people emailed for $500 sounds fantastic ("if only 3% buy my product...") Resist the temptation. The only email list you should use when you're starting out is your own.

• Link exchanges, link farms, etc. These sites will post an organic–looking link for a fee (or sometimes for free, in return for you accepting links from them). Like emailings, these should be treated with suspicion. Remember, search engines want to give value to searchers, and these exchanges are meant to artificially inflate site rankings without adding real value. So search engines hate them, and they are quite happy to make life miserable for anyone caught using them. Frankly, any site thinking they can outwit Google or Bing is taking a real chance – and if you work with them, you'll be the one paying the price. Concentrate on real organic links, and let others take the fall when it comes.

Summary

There are many ways to get traffic – far more than can fit in this book – but even a few of these put into practice will make a big difference for your site. So it's important to get started as soon as possible, and then branch out. When you see that extra traffic, you'll be glad you made the effort!

Turning Your Blog Into A Success!

You've probably never heard of William Dawes, and yet he narrowly missed being really, really, famous.

No?

Then perhaps you've heard of Paul Revere?

William Dawes was the other rider that night – yet all anyone remembers is Paul Revere and HIS midnight ride.

In the book "The Tipping Point", Malcolm Gladwell points out that Paul Revere was a "connector", someone who had excellent social skills, and was capable of promoting a cause so well that people he met were encouraged to tell others, creating a "buzz". Dawes, sadly, was not the same kind of social bon vivant, didn't inspire people to tell others, and the rest, as they say, is history.

This is not unusual, unfortunately: Many people have done things, but only some have done them successfully. For instance, Henry Ford didn't invent cars, he just built them better.

When it comes to your website, building it is only one aspect. Making it a success is the other. And while we aren't all like Paul Revere, fortunately online it's a bit easier to create a "buzz"!

In fact, you can improve your site a great deal – in any category – if you work at three areas:

• Focus.

• Track.

• Test.

Let's look at the first, focus.

Succeed With Focus

Think of two Olympic runner hopefuls. One trains hard and focuses on winning a spot on the team. The other one takes a month off, and, well, I don't even have to ask who's got the better chance. Focus is vital to get onto the Olympic team, and it's vital for getting your site out there.

Online especially, focus is hard to come by. I think it's partly because the expense to set up a site is so low. The cost to start out on the Internet (the barrier to entry) makes it easy for anyone to do so. I think if it cost people $10,000 to start an online business, people would take their websites more seriously!

Another reason for focus is to avoid falling prey to the "business of the month" club. That's where you check your email and someone is offering you success, but only if you buy their report, or course, or attend their seminar, which is on buying houses in foreclosure, or offering affiliate products, or working offline, or selling on eBay, or any of a thousand different things. So you might get tempted and spend a bit of money and time trying out the product to see if you can earn with it. Meanwhile, you lose all the momentum of the first project, and you start from scratch on the new one!

This is not the way to make money online. Focus prevents you from falling into that trap.

Note that I'm not saying here that you can never learn about other techniques, or you must flog a dead horse forever. For instance, a knowledge of Adwords is useful whether you sell your own product or do affiliate sales. How to improve your ad copy is valuable no matter what business you are in. But while learning these techniques are useful, whole new businesses are not, not if you truly believe in your current business and its potential.

What can you do about focus? Focus comes when you've decided what your goal is for your blog: A book deal, to build a business, make a certain amount of income from affiliate sales, and so forth.

For instance, a book offer means you'd need to focus on your writing and building an audience. After all, nothing cements a book deal like telling a publisher you have

50,000 potential buyers visiting your blog daily!

And for an affiliate site, profits depend on funneling traffic to sales pages that are not your own. In this case, traffic obviously plays a big part, especially paid traffic, and the focus is on how to make the maximum revenue. You need traffic to your site for the lowest cost, since lower expenses mean higher profit. As well, you'll want to research the best affiliate offers to give your visitors.

How about a business? There, the focus is on getting customers, and also on retaining those customers (since a repeat customer is often far cheaper to keep around than a new one is to gain). Therefore, the goal is on building a relationship, and that usually means building your client email list.

As you can see, no matter what the site, there is an end goal. You need to know that going in, and make that your focus. And as you concentrate on how to make your online business a success, you'll soon start seeing opportunities you never thought of before.

Tracking And Testing

You focus on what to do, thereby improving your business – so why track and test? In a nutshell, because testing and tracking can give you huge benefits. Testing lets you see what different prices, offers, and content do to the bottom line, while tracking, or monitoring, is the only way you'll know what works!

Let's go back to that Olympic hopeful: Imagine if the coach never tells him how fast he ran. How could he get better? If he eats a hearty breakfast, or tries on new shoes, will he know if it makes a difference? And is it good or bad? Obviously, to succeed he needs to track his results (his finish time), and test different ways to improve it (special meals, shoes).

So too with your site. You focus on a goal, figure out what your needs are, and monitor them. Then, you can try different ways to improve them.

For example, if you're writing your way towards that book deal, you can set up tracking for page views, or visitors per post. Once you know how many people come and view each article you write, you can then use that information to test. In effect, you're trying to 'beat' your current score for viewers with new and better articles. You'll see what types of articles people come by to read most often, and then write more of the same. Or you could monitor comments, since articles that get many

---

comments tend to be more attention grabbing or controversial. You attract people to your site, and get closer to that book offer – by testing and tracking.

Or take affiliate income. Here, the goal is a better bottom line. So, you need to track what you spend on advertising against what you get as income from affiliate sales. Once you're watching (tracking) these numbers, you can test different advertising, seeing what works and what doesn't. Perhaps one product may sell for more, and give you a higher commission, but your visitors don't seem to like it. Yet another less expensive item may sell better, and actually make you more money overall. The opposite could also be true – but without some form of tracking, you'll never be sure!

For an online business, tracking is likewise simple. Either someone buys, or else you get them to sign up to your email list (for many businesses, it's easier to get a potential client to sign up for email than to buy, so many sites work on doing that first, and then use repeated emails to make the sale).

If you go the email list route, then you track subscribers instead of income. More subscribers means you've improved something – less means you need to fix something. Closely related to that is the unsubscribe rate, which is how many and how fast people remove themselves from the list; typically, this is because of something you emailed them, and can give you a clue as to which emailings will work and which won't in the future.

So Focus. Track. Test. Keep these three in mind and you can improve ANY website.

Enough with the theory: Now let's look at some specific ways to build your site into a real money maker in more detail.

Earning With AdSense

AdSense has become extremely popular in the past few years as a way to turn traffic into money with little effort. It's a real winner for many websites, since it allows you to earn income no matter what the focus of your site is. Start an affiliate site, and until you find quality big–ticket items to offer, AdSense gives you some income; if your goal is a writing career, AdSense can make the blog profitable until a publisher comes along with their checkbook; and so on. It's well worth a look for many people.

What I like about AdSense is the anonymity of it. That is, you set up a site, put up articles, and money comes in, without having to put much of yourself out there. In contrast, if you sell a report you wrote, or offer a product or service of your own, then you're right out there actively promoting, advertising, selling. But a website can be much more passive with AdSense – just create a blog, fill with content, insert AdSense, and repeat!

As you can imagine, for AdSense sites it's a numbers game. If for example the AdSense income from a site you create is $1 per day consistently, then you've made $30 in a month. Obviously, you'll want to improve that. There are many ways to do so, but they fall into five main areas:

• More Sites.

• More Pages.

• More Clicks.

• More Money Per Click.

• More Traffic.

Obviously with the first item, more sites means more income. Using our example, one site is pocket change, but 100 sites like it will get $3,000 a month – a much more respectable amount. WordPress has spawned a whole sub–industry to aid in setting up large groups of blogs fast, since it's one of the easiest ways to get full–featured and powerful sites up rapidly. Using these techniques, 100 sites is not a problem (although finding all that new content may be!)

Beside more sites, you can choose to increase your site size with more pages: Just as 100 sites can boost your income, if that one site instead has 100 times the content, your AdSense income will go up.

Testing Your Ads For More Money

The third item, more clicks, focuses on visitors rather than your site. Instead of building up the content, the goal is to make each page 'work' harder. In AdSense, the click through ratio (CTR) is very important. You will hear people talk of 3% CTR, and others of 10% CTR or higher. CTR refers to the ratio of ad viewers to those who actually click on it; so a 10% CTR means that for every 200 people seeing the ad, 20 clicked.

Increasing the CTR with AdSense is part psychology and part testing. For example, some people have placed images near their ads to attract the eye. Google also recommends a "hot spot" for viewing, which is the top left corner of the web page.

Ad coloring is likewise important. Many sites change the border around the ads to the background color, making it invisible. Setting links to the traditional blue helps as well. Even though blue underlined links seem 'old', they are familiar, and familiar means people are more likely to click on them.

As well, shape may matter. For some sites, a long thin ad can work. For others, squarer ads work better. Some sites use vivid colors for the ad to stand out, while others use subdued colors to make the ad less 'ad–like'. The choices seem endless, and this is where testing different styles on your own web pages can reveal the real money–makers.

As always, when you make changes to the ad style, note them, and keep track of the results for each. In this way, you can have a quick display of their CTR, and see how your sites are performing. You can also use channels for different ad styles, to compare and test them.

Is there any one best AdSense ad style? Unfortunately no. A kid's site would likely do well with bright ad colors (florescent even), while a financial site could lose clicks that way. The only sure way is to set up ads on your site, and monitor the results; then change and monitor again. However, I have found some consistent items over the years: Ads that are close to the articles (both in position and in style) work best, and borderless ads do well. Coloring for the text can match the text and background color of the blog page, with the exception of the links – the URL link should be the common 'blue' we all know and love (and click on). Use these suggestions as a starting point for your ads, but remember to test!

For example, I once visited some of my poorer performing sites, and made a few adjustments, such as changing ad shapes, and placing them closer to the blog content instead of off to the side. The result? My CTR tripled! Simple tweaking like that can make your site much more profitable with only a small investment of time.

Another way to improve revenue is making each click count more. This is done by improving the value of clicks on a site – usually by better site focusing, or setting up sites based on higher–priced keywords.

Perhaps you've heard of Mesothelioma? At one time, people were talking about the cost per click of this search term involving asbestos–related lung cancer, paid by legal groups hoping to gather people into class action suits. For a while, people were setting up AdSense sites filled with articles on the topic, hoping for that $100 click (or more). While you likely won't get a $100 click now, you can see the benefits of picking valuable keywords to base your site on.

As the final item in the list, more traffic is an obvious boost, since ten times the traffic could yield ten times the clicks, and therefore ten times the income. However, not all traffic is created equal, and the temptation may be to pay for those extra visitors. While normally not a problem, on an AdSense site you are dealing with an uncertain earning amount, at least at first, so it's very easy to pay too much for the traffic. Until you're confident with your CTR, I'd recommend not going this route.

AdSense is definitely one of the biggest games in town – but it isn't the only one. So what other alternatives are there?

Other Affiliate Income

Basically, affiliate income is selling on straight commission. AdSense is an example of that, and a very simple one. But there are many, many other places that would love to have you advertise their product and give you a commission on sales.

These alternatives are especially great when AdSense doesn't cut it. For example:

• You can't get permission to use AdSense.

• Your blog doesn't suit AdSense, or the keyword focus of your site attracts very low–paying ads.

• You already have something in mind to offer.

• You've been naughty, and Google banned you.

For example, eBay has their own affiliate program. With it, you send visitors to eBay, and depending on what they do, you get a commission. Another example is Clickbank.

Clickbank is a company known for affiliate products, much of which are digital reports. You send people there, and if they buy, you likewise get a commission. The variety is huge, with many kinds of products to offer people. In fact, their products are mainly created by individuals like you; so an alternate way to earn is to create your own report and sell it via ClickBank, letting other websites get a commission from you to do all the "heavy lifting".

If you haven't picked a product or affiliate program already, or if you're looking for something new, here's a list of some of the better and/or more popular ones:

eBay: With the huge selection on eBay, there is something for everyone.

    https://partnernetwork.ebay.com/

Amazon: The biggest store online (or anywhere!) Join here to earn commissions on all their products.

    https://affiliate-program.amazon.com

ClickBank: Digital products for the most part, and also a great place to offer any products you make.

    https://www.clickbank.com/affiliate-network/

Commission Junction: Many companies have C.J. run their affiliate program, so joining this one can open the door for a wide variety of products.

    http://www.cj.com/

For each, be sure to visit their site and check into the current signup details. If one or more of them is a good fit, then join, and place their ads on your site.

One note: Compared to AdSense, many of these companies have somewhat limited options for advertising. For example, Commission Junction lets you look through a list of ads from companies, and pick the ones you want; but unlike AdSense, there is little ad customization. This can make things easier for you, but at the cost of being less flexible. On the other hand, the commissions for some of these products can be much higher than a typical AdSense click.

The advantage of sites like these is that they deal with all the affiliate details, and just send you your payment regularly (often by check or a deposit to your PayPal account). Definitely for a first–timer, these are the best ones to get your feet wet with when trying out affiliate programs.

Profiting With List Building

"The money is in the list." Everyone, without exception, recommends that online businesses build an email list – often as a first priority.

List building is valuable because you are creating a relationship with a group of people that want to hear from you regularly (and if they don't, they WILL quit the list). This relationship is great for promotion, whether it is for a product sale, or to encourage them to buy your book, or even to offer an affiliate item in an email. For this reason, I recommend working on an email list for just about any site.

List building can be simple: The people on the site are enticed to sign up to your list, the promise of getting 'something' making them part with their email address. That offer then is the key to building a large list. It should both relate to your site niche and be worthwhile. Providing an email address is awkward these days. I regularly pass up offers because I anticipate garbage email and spam, so an offer has to be especially interesting to get me to share my address. I'm not alone, so make your offer valuable and you'll get responses.

One more thing: Don't forget to assure them their email is safe and secure while you're at it – and check your mailing list's website to comply with any legal requirements to do so.

Another aspect of list building is regularity, emailing the list frequently to build a relationship. While not always easy (finding something to say at the beginning is hard), a useful technique is to set aside a specific day each week, and write on a topic you find interesting and that relates to your site. If nothing else, consider a summary of your site for the week, with links to the articles. But keep it consistent.

As well, be real. You're emailing real people, and you are a real person. Avoid jargon, be sincere and honest, and understand that these people are busy and have their own lives; they simply want worthwhile information and help. It will show in your writing – and will improve your results.

But don't be afraid to sell. Your list exists to sell. Your subscribers should realize this. And frankly, if they don't, you might as well have them leave, since they are not going to make you any money. So take opportunities in your emails to sell. Don't make it the only purpose for each and every email, since that tends to get people unsubscribing quickly, but make sure it appears as a part of each email if possible.

These are just a few tips for email lists. The subject of email has been discussed in great detail over the years, and a quick search online will get you plenty of information and tips on creating and managing an effective email list. But before we finish off the subject, there's one more point to add, and that's avoiding the Do–It–Yourself route.

Do It Yourself Email: Problems?

I'll be blunt: Do not try to run an email list directly via your site!

In the distant past it may have been a possibility, but with all the legal issues involved today, if anything is not done properly it could cause you some really serious problems.

For this reason, I recommend a third party manager for email lists. Do a search for companies, compare the prices, and check out reviews. However, spend some time picking carefully, because you don't want to move services after you are up and running. Changing requires people to sign up to your list a second time, something very few will end up doing. I've lost as many as 80% of my list members by transferring between email services, and others have reported the same problem. So pick a good company and stay with them (and if you're stuck on where to start, the one I use is called Aweber.com, and I'm quite satisfied with them; I've also heard good things about Mailchimp.com)

Summary

Looking at these options, you'll see there are many ways to leverage your WordPress blog (or blogs) for success. Quite likely you already have a goal in mind, so some of these may be more useful than others. But no matter how you "go for it", and what your blog is destined for, remember the three keys: Focus, Test, and Track.

Set your blog up, stick with it, and progressively try new things, keeping the winning ideas. Do that, and your site is bound to improve – and You WILL Succeed!

Conclusion

I hope you've enjoyed this book, and that it's provided you a good grounding in online business building, and using WordPress to attain your goals.

Despite these economic times, the Internet has made it easier than ever to make money, and without any physical product at all. The Internet has little cost to join, and if you can get enough people to pay attention to your message, you can actually make money from digital 'dust' – absolutely nothing but electrons.

That means that anyone with an idea has a real chance of earning money – and that 'anyone' can well be YOU!

I hope this book's information has given you a start in your education for money–making on the Internet, and how best to build a business on it. I firmly believe that with the right idea, and of course WordPress (plus this book, I immodestly add), you'll have the tools to make a thriving business online.

To Your Future Success!

David Pankhurst

About The Author

Besides writing on technical subjects like WordPress, David Pankhurst also blogs at his site http://www.UtopiaMechanicus.com/ which is itself a modified WordPress site. Since 2004, he has been an avid fan and supporter of WordPress.

Index

www.ingramcontent.com/pod-product-compliance
Lightning Source LLC
Chambersburg PA
CBHW081727220526
45468CB00008B/2003